WALKS & TOURS

LISBON

YOUR TAILOR-MADE TRIP STARTS HERE

Tailor-made trips and unique adventures crafted by local experts

Rough Guides has been inspiring travellers with lively and thought-provoking guidebooks for more than 35 years. Now we're linking you up with selected local experts to craft your dream trip. They will put together your perfect itinerary and book it at local rates.

Don't follow the crowd – find your own path.

HOW ROUGHGUIDES.COM/TRIPS WORKS

STEP 1

Pick your dream destination, tell us what you want and submit an enquiry.

STEP 2

Fill in a short form to tell your local expert about your dream trip and preferences.

STEP 3

Our local expert will craft your tailor-made itinerary. You'll be able to tweak and refine it until you're completely satisfied.

STEP 4

Book online with ease, pack your bags and enjoy the trip! Our local expert will be on hand 24/7 while you're on the road.

BENEFITS OF PLANNING AND BOOKING AT ROUGHGUIDES.COM/TRIPS

PLAN YOUR ADVENTURE WITH LOCAL EXPERTS

Rough Guides' English-speaking local experts are hand-picked, based on their experience in the travel industry and their impeccable standards of customer service.

SAVE TIME AND GET ACCESS TO LOCAL KNOWLEDGE

When a local expert plans your trip, you save time and money when you book, even during high season. You won't be charged for using a credit card either.

MAKE TRAVEL A BREEZE: BOOK WITH PEACE OF MIND

Enjoy stress-free travel when you use Rough Guides' secure online booking platform. All bookings come with a money-back guarantee.

WHAT DO OTHER TRAVELLERS THINK ABOUT ROUGH GUIDES TRIPS?

Trip to Spain

This Spain tour company did a fantastic job to make our dream trip perfect. We gave them our travel budget, told them where we would like to go, and they did all of the planning. Our drivers and tour guides were always on time and very knowledgable. The hotel accommodations were better than we would have found on our own. Only one time did we end up in a location that we had not intended to be in. We called the 24 hour phone number, and they immediately fixed the situation.

Don A, USA

Trip to Morocco

Our trip was fantastic! Transportation, accommodations, guides – all were well chosen! The hotels were well situated, well appointed and had helpful, friendly staff. All of the guides we had were very knowledgeable, patient, and flexible with our varied interests in the different sites. We particularly enjoyed the side trip to Tangier! Well done! The itinerary you arranged for us allowed maximum coverage of the country with time in each city for seeing the important places.

Sharon, USA

PLAN AND BOOK YOUR TRIP AT
ROUGHGUIDES.COM/TRIPS

CONTENTS

Art buffs

Don't miss the treasures in the Gulbenkian (walk 4), the masterpieces in the Museu Nacional de Arte Antiga (walk 5) and the modern and contemporary art at the Museu de Arte Contemporânea (tour 6).

Best walks & tours for...

Castles and palaces

Explore Lisbon's Castelo de São Jorge (walk 1), visit the palaces of Mafra and Queluz (tours 13 and 14), or the Moorish castle ruins and fantasy palaces of Sintra (tour 10).

Fans of the Manueline

Hop on a tram to Belém to see the district's famous monuments: the Mosteiro dos Jerónimos and Torre de Belém (tour 6); and if in Setúbal (tour 12), don't miss the remarkable Convento de Jesus.

Foodies

Good restaurants are springing up all around the city but for some of the most memorable dining experiences, try the family-run *tascas* hidden away in the back alleys of Bairro Alto (walk 3) or Alfama (walk 1).

Night owls

Join the revellers in bohemian Bairro Alto (walk 3) or party the night away in trendy Cais do Sodré (walk 2). For *fado* head to Alfama (walk 1) or Mouraria.

Shoppers

Explore the streets of Baixa (walk 2) to discover a fast-disappearing breed of quirky, old-fashioned stores, Chiado (walk 3) for smart Art Deco shops and Bairro Alto (also walk 3) for vintage finds and independent boutiques.

Families with children

Europe's third-largest oceanarium (walk 7) should be top of the agenda. Climb up and down hills on the rattling Tram 28 (tour 9), cross the river to the Cristo Rei (tour 8) or have fun on the beach (tour 11).

Dazzling views

For fine city and river views head up to the *miradouros* (viewpoints) such as the Castle Belvedere, Portas do Sol, Miradouro da Santa Luzia (walk 1) or Miradouro de São Pedro de Alcântara (walk 3).

INTRODUCTION

An introduction to Lisbon and what makes it special, what not to miss and what to do when you're there.

Discover Lisbon

With its sunny climate, rich history and old-world charm, Lisbon has an enduring appeal. Add gastronomy, nightlife and relatively affordable prices and it is little wonder the Portuguese capital has become one of Europe's tourist hotspots.

Located on the broad estuary of the River Tagus where it spills into the Atlantic, Lisbon is Europe's most westerly capital. The city's arching waterfront stretches nearly 32km (21 miles) along the river. Towards the Atlantic is Belém, launching point for Vasco da Gama and other explorers of the Age of Discovery, and at the eastern extreme is the Parque das Nações, site of Expo 98. Between the two is central Lisbon: the kasbah-like Alfama topped by the Moorish castle, the quintessential hilltop Bairro Alto and in the middle, downtown Baixa, elegantly rebuilt in the eighteenth century after one of the worst earthquakes ever recorded.

Geography and layout

Much of Lisbon's appeal lies in its location. Spread across seven hills, the city offers myriad *miradouros* (lookout points) affording spectacular views over a sprawl of terracotta roof tiles to the placid Tagus. Two of the largest bridges in Europe leap across the estuary, an expanse of water so wide it evokes a sense of the sea. Just past the district of Belém, where Manueline monuments stand sentient as symbols of Portugal's Golden Age.

Any map shows that many of the city's top attractions are within walking distance of the river, but because of the hills and the way in which the sights are spread out, it isn't always easy to travel directly from one to another. Locals carry bags of bread and groceries up and down Lisbon's hills without complaint, even in mid-summer, and tourists who wander on foot are rewarded with picturesque nooks or brilliant panoramas. Public transport, however, is inexpensive and, most of the time, efficient. Vintage trams rattle their way around the old town; funiculars make light work of steep slopes; the metro is modern and fast; buses straightforward; and taxis or tuk-tuks plentiful.

The routes in this Guide first explore the diverse neighbourhoods of the city centre, then focus on outlying areas, particularly Belém. But quaint districts, a beautiful skyline and monuments to former splendour are not the end of the capital's charms. Lisbon is surrounded by some of Portugal's most appealing destinations, most of them easily reached by public transport. For those

Lisbon's famous sights are best seen by tram

with time to venture beyond the city, there are trips west to magical Sintra, where palaces and *quintas* (estates) stud beautiful pine-clad hills, or to the sparkling resorts of the Cascais coast and the Atlantic-battered beaches to the north. Over the Tagus to the south those with a car can explore the wild Serra da Arrábida. Further north lies the monumental palace-convent of Mafra; closer to the capital, the handsome Versailles-style palace at Queluz is another major draw for visitors, including heads of state.

Climate

Although the cold Atlantic lies only a few kilometres downriver, Lisbon feels decidedly Mediterranean. A sheltered, south-facing location and mild winters allow palm trees and bird-of-paradise flowers to flourish, and the balmy weather encourages an unhurried pace. It is a year-round destination but the best times to visit the city are spring and autumn, when temperatures are pleasant, there are fewer crowds than summer and plenty of cultural activities. May and October are ideal. Summers can be very hot, but you can always cool off on nearby beaches. Temperatures normally remain warm until November and even in winter it can still be mild and sunny.

Population

The biggest city in Portugal, Lisbon is home to around 570,000 people in the centre, with over three million throughout greater Lisbon – making up about thirty percent of Portugal's total population. Despite the inescapable presence of its storied past, this is a modern, cosmopolitan capital whose streets teem with people of diverse ethnicity. Many are migrants from Portugal's former African colonies – Angola, Cape Verde, Mozambique, Brazil, Macau and Goa

The Great Earthquake

On 1 November 1755 a massive earthquake shook the whole of Europe and ripped through the city of Lisbon. It was All Saints' Day and churches were packed with crowds. Buildings crumbled, fires spread, and the waters of the Tagus heaved into a tidal wave which steamrollered the port and lower town with devastating force. The triple disaster is estimated to have killed between 15,000 and 60,000 of the 270,000 residents. Yet Lisbon grew again in grace and stature under the guiding hand of the already powerful Marquês de Pombal, chief minister to the ineffective and profligate King José I. His methods were tough, ambitious and tyrannical but in the following twenty years or so he masterminded Portugal's reconstruction from the ruins. The Neoclassical architectural style of the Baixa was rapidly dubbed 'pombalina'.

Museu da Cerveja

Ornate tiles in Restauradores metro

The Golden Age

Lisbon's gaze was always fixed firmly out to sea. Once a remote outpost of what was thought to be the farthest edge of the known world, by the fifteenth century the town had become the centre of Portuguese exploration. It was from Lisbon that Vasco da Gama set out on his voyage in the summer of 1497, reaching Calicut in southern India the following year. Portugal put paid to the Venetian monopoly of the Eastern spice trade by seizing control of the Indian Ocean and attracting merchants from all over Europe to Lisbon. Further territories were "discovered" when Pedro Álvares Cabral reached Brazil in 1500, and Lisbon was converted from a European backwater into a wealthy world city. Even after the catastrophic earthquake of 1755, no expense was spared in rebuilding. As Lisbon is one of the few European capitals to have survived the continent's twentieth-century wars unscathed, many of the historic buildings remain intact, an enduring testimony to a prosperous and glorious past.

– adding dialects, dishes and cultures to the city's makeup. In recent years, an influx of migrants from the USA and Northern Europe and wealthy remote workers have arrived, bringing economic, housing and social changes.

Local customs

Through the centuries Lisbon has offered shelter to Europe's outcasts, becoming a haven for exiles and a last refuge to monarchs who had lost their thrones. Today, the capital continues its tradition of extending a warm welcome to visitors. And of all Portugal's friends, none have endured as long as the English. The Anglo-Portuguese Alliance, ratified at the Treaty of Windsor in 1386, is the longest continuing alliance in world history. Many Lisboetas speak English, and you will unlikely have any problem being understood in hotels and restaurants, though mastering some Portuguese is always hugely appreciated.

Eating out in the city is a way of life. The Portuguese love both food and socialising, and one of the great joys of visiting Lisbon is the gastronomy and wine on offer, whether they are enjoyed at a family-run *tasca*, beachside *taberna* or one of the capital's chic designer restaurants and bars. Local cooking owes much to Portugal's close ties to the sea. Fresh fish and seafood are abundant – as is the much-loved but imported *bacalhau* (cod fish).

If you want buzz by night – and there is plenty of it – start the evening late. Many restaurants don't come to life until around 9pm and it's around this time that the powerful and soulful strains of *fado* beckon from the streets of Alfama and Mouraria. Meanwhile, Lisbon's bars and club scene thrives until the early hours.

Fado, the soulful sound of Lisbon

Don't leave Lisbon without......

Reaching the dizzy heights. Take a lift or tram to one of Lisbon's many *miradouros* (viewpoints) for unforgettable vistas of the city and river.

Sampling custard tarts *(pastéis de nata).* Discover these culinary delights at virtually any café, bakery or *pasteleria*, but ideally at *Pastéis de Belém* which sells well over 20,000 a day, warm from the oven. See page 17.

Taking a trip on a tram. Hop on any vintage tram (No 28 is the best known) and enjoy views of Lisbon's iconic landmarks as it rattles up and down the city's steep hills. See page 74.

Try *bacalhau.* The Portuguese have created some delicious dishes with their beloved dried salted cod. There are said to be 365 recipes – one for every day of the year. Sample it in one of the family restaurants tucked away in the backstreets of Alfama. See page 17.

Bar-hopping in the Bairro Alto. Sleepy by day, the Bairro Alto springs to life after dark. By 11pm, the lanes take on a carnival street-party vibe. Follow the flow to buzzy bars and nightclubs, some open until 5am. See page 43.

Time Out Mercado da Ribeira. This hugely successful gourmand haven is packed with over forty food kiosks serving cuisine from leading Portuguese chefs. Whatever local speciality you want to try, this is the place to come. See page 117.

Experience *fado.* Listen to the soulful strands of *fado*, Portugal's musical expression of longing and sorrow. Many places offer an evening of *fado* accompanied with food and wine. See page 23.

Back alleys of Alfama. Duck down the labyrinthine backstreets of Moorish Alfama, which retains a village-like atmosphere. See page 28.

Coastal charms. Leave the bustle of the city behind, hop on a train and head for the Cascais coast for sandy beaches tousled by the cooling Atlantic breeze. See page 85.

A cherry fix. Join the locals around Largo de São Domingos at one of the little *ginjinha* bars. A shot of this affordable sweet liqueur comes with or without cherries and is sometimes served in a chocolate cup. See page 40.

Local economy

Once the poorest EU country in Western Europe, Lisbon has benefitted hugely from EU investment and emerged an altered, enlarged and dynamic city. As hosts of Expo 98, the world fair held on the 500th anniversary of Vasco da Gama's discovery of the sea route to India, Lisbon launched a brand-new neighbourhood, the Parque das Nações. A derelict industrial site was reimagined as an

The Ponte 25 de Abril

ahead-of-the-curve site of innovative buildings, a giant oceanarium, and over the Tagus, the gleaming 17km (10.6 mile) Ponte de Vasco da Gama, the longest bridge in Europe.

Ten years on, the financial crisis of 2008 left Portugal with a spiralling budget deficit. In 2011 it became the third European country, after Greece and Ireland, to ask for a financial bailout (€78 bn) from the EU. It wasn't until 2014, after a string of harsh austerity measures, that Portugal exited the bailout programme. Since then, the Portuguese economy has undergone a significant recovery. Tourism has been one of the main drivers. Lisbon now sees around fifteen million foreign visitors annually, thanks in part to climate and affordable prices – it was one of the cheapest cities in Western Europe, though prices are fast increasing. It has also become a popular stop for cruise ships.

Recent years have witnessed a boom in new hotels and restaurants along with an ever-growing tech and entrepreneurial scene. Crumbling buildings in the city centre, abandoned for years, have been snapped up by foreigners attracted by Portugal's tax-friendly programmes. This has helped turn Portugal into Western Europe's second-hottest property market but has also meant that many locals, unable to afford soaring house prices and rising rents in Lisbon (and Porto), have deserted the cities.

Lisbon today

Lisbon's contemporary culture is thriving. Former ignored areas have become hip neighbourhoods, with urban art, cool boutiques and galleries promoting all things Portuguese. Previously overlooked districts have been revitalised by a wave of new cultural hubs, including the 2016-opened Museum of Art, Architecture and Technology (MAAT) and 2023's big-hitter, 8 Marvila, a cluster of historic wine warehouses turned into shops and restaurants. Old quays and warehouses have been transformed into lively hubs of activity, buzzing from day to night. The waterfront west of the main Praça do Comércio, now has a diminutive beach and an inviting promenade for walking, cycling or just sitting on a deckchair watching boats glide by.

Despite its dramatic and fast transformation into one of Europe's most dynamic capitals, Lisbon has managed to retain the feel of a laid-back provincial capital, with its narrow Moorish-style streets, beautiful hand-painted *azulejos* (tiles) and occasional ornate architectural flourish. Historic village-like neighbourhoods have clung onto their quirky charm, vintage trams continue to crank up and down steep hills, washing flaps on crumbling facades and old-timers still enjoy a *bica* (espresso) or tot of *ginginja* in the city's many traditional cafés and bars. Lisbon has changed with the times, but its old-world charm is never far away.

Lisbon's hills viewed from Sao Pedro de Alcantara

Top tips for visiting Lisbon

Tickets. If you plan to visit multiple attractions, the good-value Lisboa Card, available online at www.shop.visitlisboa.com, entitles you to free metro, bus, tram and lift transport, admission to 51 sights (including some outside Lisbon) plus discounts on tours, a complimentary tourist guide and free travel by train to Sintra and Cascais. The card is available for 24, 48 and 72 hours and costs €27, €44 and €72, respectively. Remember that most museums close on Mondays.

Free appetisers. Most restaurants serve unrequested appetisers known as *couvert*, such as bread, olives, cheese and fish pâtés, that appear to be free. They are not. You will be expected to pay a few euros for each, though you can politely decline any or all items and then will not be charged.

Market price. If you see *'preco V'* (or simply 'PV') beside seafood on a menu, it means the price is variable depending on that day's market price. Ask the fee before ordering.

Cheap eats. To fill up for around €12, opt for the *ementa turística*, a daily changing set menu, including coffee and a drink. The *prato do dia* is the dish of the day, often a good-value choice.

Musical offerings. Keep an ear out for concerts as you stroll around the streets and your eyes peeled for posters and flyers advertising them. Look out for free events, such as performances at Castelo São Jorge in summer and the Gulbenkian Museum, and open-air gigs from June to September.

Reserve a table. As the best restaurants are often both cramped and coveted by Lisboetas, call at least a day in advance to secure a table. At weekends this is essential.

Follow Me Lisboa. This free monthly booklet, available at tourist offices and online at www.visitlisboa.com, includes up-to-date opening hours and other information on all the main sights, as well as details on nightlife, restaurants and transport.

Tram tips. Lisbon's much-loved trams are packed with tourists. To ensure a seat, take the tram from its departure point rather than trying to alight along the route.

The hidden price of people-watching. An increasing number of cafés, particularly those in the famous squares, have started charging extra for table service. But in neighbourhood haunts, you still pay the same whether it's a drink at the bar or on the terrace.

Free tickets. The famous Calouste Gulbenkian Museum is free on Sunday after 2pm. For walking tours at no charge (except a tip), visit www.hilisbonwalkingtours.com.

Food and drink

Choose from trusty hole-in-the-wall *tascas*, riverside or beach seafood restaurants, retro bistros or new culinary hotspots where creative chefs give Portuguese cuisine a contemporary twist.

Local food is usually fresh, filling and full of flavour; and if you avoid the tourist traps you can eat well and cheaply. With its river setting and proximity to the sea, the city has a wonderful abundance of fish and seafood. Visit any fish market and you will see a gleaming array of squid *(lula)*, cuttlefish *(choco)*, octopus *(polvo)* sea bass *(robalo)*, gilthead bream *(dourada)*, sardines *(sardinhas)* and shellfish such as oysters *(ostras)*, clams *(ameijoas)* and lobster *(lagosta)*.

Flavours from China, India, Brazil and Africa reflect Portugal's colonial past. The former colony of Goa accounts for the local popularity of *caril* (curry) and other Indian-style dishes. *Piri-piri*, often served with chicken, is a hot chilli sauce from Angola that will set most mouths ablaze. Four centuries of ties with Macau assures all lovers of Chinese food a night out with dishes such as *gambas doces* (sweet-and-sour prawns).

Places to eat

Tascas, mainly found in the narrow streets of Baixa, Alfama and Bairro Alto, are traditionally tiny, family-run joints serving hearty helpings of authentic Portuguese cuisine. A *churrasqueira* is a grill, typically unassuming with paper tablecloths, serving fare like grilled sardines or half-chicken. A *marisqueira* specialises in seafood; a *cervejaria* is a beer house, but normally serves seafood and steaks as well. A *restaurante* spans a whole range of eateries, from sumptuous to basic. The tourist menu *(ementa turística)* offered by some restaurants, particularly at lunchtime, changes daily and can be excellent value. Lisbon has a vibrant café culture, with a staggering number of places offering the simple pleasure of relaxing over a cup of good coffee and a freshly made pastry. Dotted around the city are dark-green kiosks offering snacks and drinks at reasonable prices, some sited on hills with fantastic views.

For markets see page 116.

What to eat

No sooner are you seated than pre-starters *(couvert)* of bread, butter, cheese, olives, fish pâté or cured ham will appear on the table. These are optional and there is nearly always a charge. It may only be a couple of euros for bread or

Porco à alentejana, pork and clams with paprika

olives, but it could be €5 or more for the cheese or meat. It's perfectly acceptable to decline them without charge.

Soups and starters

Starters are typically seafood (see below), speciality hams and cheeses, or hale-and-hearty soups. *Caldo verde*, a kale and potato soup, sometimes with chunks of sausage, is served everywhere from the classiest restaurant to the humblest *tasca*. A similar dish is *sopa à Portuguesa* but with added broccoli, turnips, beans, carrots and anything else the cook happens to have to hand. Thick bread soups include *açorda à Alentejana*, with coriander, garlic and whole poached eggs, and *açorda de marisco*, a spicy, garlicky shellfish broth. Other starters are cured and smoked hams, or sausages and salamis, often heavily smoked and spiced.

Fish and seafood

Seafood restaurants often sell shellfish by the weight, giving the price in euros per kilo. Local seafood specialities include *caldeirada de peixe*, a rich seafood stew; *arroz de marisco*, a delicious rice dish with crab, lobster claws, prawns, clams and cockles; *ameijoas na cataplana*, steamed clams with chorizo or another type of pork, tomato, white wine, ham, onion and herbs. Clams are often served simply with crushed garlic cloves and fresh coriander: *amêijoas à bulhão pato*. Squid, stuffed with rice, olives, tomato, onion and herbs, is known as *lulas recheadas*, though large squid is often grilled and served on a skewer *(espetada)* with prawns *(gambas)*. Fish normally comes simply grilled. You can't tell from the menu whether it's fresh or frozen, so ask the waiter for the catch of the day. And don't assume the bass and bream is from the high seas – much of it is farmed these days.

Secret tarts

You can't visit Lisbon and not sample the *pastéis de Belém*, creamy custard tarts made to a special and, of course, secret recipe. The tarts, generically known as *pastéis de nata*, can be found all over the city but those from the *Pastéis de Belém* (see page 66) are the crème de la crème. The story goes that they used to be made by the monks of the Jerónimos Monastery, just a few steps away, and that when the monasteries were dissolved in the 1830s the recipe was passed on to a local baker. It is also said that only three bakers at any one time know the recipe, which they pass on to someone else on retirement.

The national dish

The Portuguese passion for *bacalhau*, dried salted cod, fished in distant seas, may seem strange in a city on a river and close to the ocean with so much fresh fish available. But you come across *bacalhau* everywhere and the Portuguese

Custard tarts, *Pastéis de Belém*

Portuguese cheese

Food and drink prices

Throughout this Guide, the price categories for a two-course meal for one with a glass of house wine are:

€€€€ = over €60
€€€ = €35–60
€€ = €20–35
€ = under €20

claim to have 365 ways of preparing it, one for every day of the year. There are many savoury ways the local staple can be prepared, such as *bacalhau à gomes de sá* (casseroled with potato, onion and olives) or *à brás* (flaked with fried potato, onion, egg, parsley and topped with black olives). If you just want a taste, try one of the *pastéis de bacalhau*, delicious little salt-cod croquettes. *Bacalhau* is usually accompanied with red rather than white wine.

Meat dishes

Although fish and seafood predominate on menus and is the best thing to try, restaurants do not skimp on meat. You can find excellent pork dishes, often roasted or served in robust stews, as well as chicken, steak, braised rabbit and wild boar. Be sure to try *porco à alentejana*, pork and clams spiced with paprika. *Feijoada*, a hearty stew of white beans, vegetables and meat, usually includes pork of some sort, typically pigs' trotters and sausage. If you want to splash out, try the delicious *leitão assado* (roast suckling pig) in one of the more expensive restaurants.

Chicken *(frango)* is popular and prepared in many ways but most commonly found as *frango piri-piri*, when it is marinaded and barbecued to a tasty crisp with chilli oil. *Bife à portuguesa* is steak in a gravy-like sauce, topped with ham, thin potatoes and occasionally an egg; *pregos* are small steak sandwiches.

From April to September, you'll see restaurants displaying signs saying '*há caracóis*' where locals will be tucking into platters of tiny snails, washed down with icy Sagres. The molluscs are an easy catch (they travel at around five metres an hour), are highly nutritious and very low in calories.

Desserts

The Portuguese have a sweet tooth, and Lisbon is packed with *pastelerias* (patisseries), bakeries and cafés selling delicious cakes and pastries. The favourites are the *pastéis de nata* (custard tarts), eaten with coffee any time of day or as a dessert in almost every restaurant and café (see box). Other options are *pudim flan*, the Portuguese version of crème caramel; *arroz doce*, a lemon-flavoured rice pudding sprinkled with cinnamon; and *pudim molotov*, fluffy egg-white mousse in a pool of sticky caramel sauce. You may also come across so-called 'convent sweets', as they were made by nuns in the eighteenth century to raise money. One of the more readily

Simply served fresh prawns

available is a confection called *toucinho do ceu*, 'food from heaven', made from sugar, almonds and egg yolks.

Cheese

If you still have space after dessert, sample some Portuguese cheese. The richest and most expensive is *Serra da Estrela*, made from cured ewe's milk cheese which originates high up in the mountains and can be served fresh or cured. Some restaurants serve *queijo fresco* (fresh cheese) as an appetiser. This is usually a small, white, soft cheese made of ewe's and goat's milk.

Wine

Portuguese table wine has come on in leaps and bounds in recent years. Try the good-value Alentejo wines, available everywhere in Lisbon. The Douro Valley, traditionally renowned for port, now produces robust and full-bodied reds, as well as some interesting whites. The Dão region to the south is also behind some of the country's finest reds. *Vinho verde* (green wine) is a refreshing, slightly sparkling young wine, which goes well with seafood.

Fortified port wine has tantalised palates around the world since the British began exporting it in the seventeenth century. An easy if touristy place in Lisbon to sample port wines is the *Solar do Vinho do Porto* (see page 44). Port and Madeira, the two most celebrated Portuguese wines, are mostly known as postprandial dessert wines but may also be sipped as aperitifs. The before-dinner varieties are dry and extra-dry white port and the dry Madeiras, Sercial and Verdelho. These should be served slightly chilled. Alternatively try a P&T, *porto tónico* (dry white port and tonic), which is currently having a moment as a summer cocktail. After dinner, sip one of the famous tawny ports (the aged varieties are especially good), or a Madeira dessert wine, Boal or Malvasia (also known as Malmsey).

Other drinks

Portuguese beers are good and refreshing. Light or dark, they are served chilled, bottled or from the tap. The main brands are Sagres and Super Bock, though craft breweries now thrive in Lisbon.

A favourite Portuguese tipple is *ginjinha* (or *ginja*), a sweet and potent cherry liqueur, which comes with or without cherries. It originated in Lisbon and was once seen as a miracle cure for all manner of illnesses. You'll find it all over town, but most characteristically in the small *ginjinha* bars around Rossio; the 1840-founded *A Ginjinha* does a roaring trade.

Coffee

Coffee is a way of life for the Portuguese. The most popular form is *uma bica*, a small, strong espresso; a weaker version is a *carioca*, with a drop of milk is a *garoto*. If you want plenty of milk with your coffee, ask for a *galão*.

Dourada for sale at the Mercado da Ribeira

Shopping

In Lisbon, young designers showing off their latest creations rub shoulders with old-fashioned stores that appear to have hardly altered in hundred years.

The Chiado district is the place to go for vintage clothes, jewellery, interiors and smart designer wear. It is home to the swish Armazéns do Chiado shopping centre and the elegant cafés and stores lining Rua Garrett, including the Bertrand bookshop, dating back to 1732.

For antique shops, hip boutiques and cutting-edge designers head to Príncipe Real. Embaixada (www.embaixadalx.pt) is a spectacular nineteenth-century neo-Arab palace converted into a hip shopping gallery focusing on avant-garde Portuguese design, arts and crafts, fashion and culture.

The central grid of streets around Rua Augusta in the Baixa shelters some wonderfully atmospheric shops selling traditional foods, clothing and jewellery, though Rua Augusta itself has an increasing number of high-street international chains.

Made in Portugal

Portugal is famous for pottery and ceramics, found in many designs and colours from folksy earthenware to hand-painted *azulejos* (decorative tiles) and Vista Alegre fine porcelain tableware. For high-quality tiles and ceramics handmade using traditional techniques head to the Sant'Anna factory (www.santanna.com.pt) in Belém or its Chiado showroom. Also in Chiado, A Vida Portuguesa (www.avidaportuguesa.com) is an enchanting late-nineteenth-century emporium with genuine Portuguese products, from retro-wrapped gourmet products to soaps, sprays, jewellery and notebooks. The large Lisbon Shop (Rua do Arsenal 7–15) in the city centre specialises in all things home-grown and is an ideal store for affordable souvenirs.

Portugal produces over half the world's cork in terms of the raw material, even more so in finished products. While an ever-growing crop of wine bottlers are using screw caps, new inventive uses are being discovered for eco-friendly cork, from bracelets and bags to lampshades, hats and handbags. Try Cork & Co (www.corkandcompany.pt) in Bairro Alto.

Gastronomy

Groceries and delicatessens have a tempting array of smoked meats, whole hams, spicy sausages and

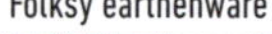
Folksy earthenware

cheeses. Manuel Tavares, between Rossio and Praça da Figueira, is one of Lisbon's oldest delis, offering fine wines and port, charcuterie, cheese and chocolates. The Conserveira de Lisboa (www.conserveiradelisboa.pt) in Baixa is a lovely old-fashioned shop lined with shelves of attractively packaged gourmet fish (tinned tuna, squid, sardines). Portugal has long been famous for its fortified port wine from the Douro Valley; try before you buy at the Solar do Vinho do Porto (see page 44).

LX Factory

In Alcântara, the cool and creative LX Factory (Rua Rodrigues Faria 103; www.lxfactory.com) beneath the Ponte 25 Abril is a former industrial estate converted into a creative enclave of workshops, art and design studios, boutiques, bars and restaurants. A lively programme of cultural events includes exhibitions, music, films – and a flea market on Sunday from noon to 7pm.

Markets

In the Campo de Santa Clara, the Feira da Ladra (Thieves' Market; Tues–Sat dawn to dusk) flea market has a large range of second-hand items and the odd dusty treasure. A collectors' market is held every Sunday morning in Cais do Sodré. The Mercado da Ribeira at Cais do Sodré has a morning food market, but the main calling card is the food court, with over thirty stalls presenting tasty eats from Portuguese top chefs. West of the centre, with fewer tourists, is the excellent Mercado de Campo Ourique, a traditional food market with a new gourmet hall.

High-end design

A wave of Portuguese designers have garnered international acclaim, and Chiado and Bairro Alto are good places to seek them out. The Portuguese leather industry is known worldwide, and jackets, belts, bags, wallets and shoes are all good-value buys. Lisbon has witnessed a boom in the luxury market in recent years. Big designer names cluster the Avenida da Liberdade.

Shopping centres

The postmodern smoky glass towers of Amoreiras (www.amoreiras.com) shelter supermarkets, cinemas, art galleries and a food court as well as two hundred shops, and (for a fee) great views from the top. The huge Centro Colombo (www.colombo.pt) has over 340 stores, while popular Spanish department store El Corte Ingles (www.elcorteingles.pt) spans everything from top designers to high-street brands and a huge supermarket. At the Parque das Nações, the glass-roofed Centro Vasco da Gama (www.centrovascodagama.pt) is filled with shops and fast-food outlets.

Rooster souvenirs

Feira da Ladra

Culture and nightlife

The Portuguese capital is a great place to party, with after-dark hangouts ranging from traditional *fado venues to* speakeasies, African nightclubs and alternative bars. Lisbon also offers a wide variety of classical concerts and occasional opera and ballet.

Lisbon's cultural scene is as diverse as you would expect from a European capital city. Its nightlife is buzzing, with bars and clubs galore, though for many Portuguese – and tourists – the classic after-hours outing in Lisbon is still to a *casa de fado* in Mouraria, Alfama or Bairro Alto. Often described as a kind of Portuguese blues, *fado* is believed to derive from music that was popular with eighteenth-century immigrants from Portugal's colonies who first settled in Alfama and today is listed on the UNESCO Intangible Cultural Heritage list.

Nightlife

When in Lisbon, do as the Lisboetas do and kickstart the evening with a glass of *ginjinha* (cherry liqueur) at one of the hole-in-the-wall bars around Rossio (see page 38). Bairro Alto positively buzzes after dark with nightclubs, jazz venues and bars spilling onto the streets, some opening as late as 11pm, and clubs even later. The night is long in Lisbon – you can dance until dawn.

More mainstream are the dock areas west of centre, where warehouses have been converted into fashionable (and relatively pricey) late-night bars and restaurants. Doca do Alcântara and Doca de Santo Amaro marina both have river-facing esplanades, popular from day to night. A more central nightlife hub is Cais do Sodré, littered with cool clubs but still retaining vestiges of its red-light past. The hip Intendente quarter, northeast of the centre, is a hub for alternative shops and cultural spaces while Marvila has seen a boom in craft-beer bars in recent years. More fanciful in style is Príncipe Real, with its trendy cocktail bars and cafés and thriving LGBTQ+ scene.

Performing arts

Look out for flyers advertising concerts in churches and palaces, some free of charge. The city's most important cultural institution is the Gulbenkian Foundation (see page 51), which maintains its own symphony orchestra and draws leading world orchestras and chamber groups. The Museu Gulbenkian (www.gulbenkian.pt) hosts recitals, classical music and dance programmes, including open-air concerts in its amphitheatre in summer. Major symphonies and

Fado in Bairro Alto

occasional opera are performed by the Portuguese Symphony Orchestra, based at the lovely Rococo opera house, the Teatro Nacional de São Carlo. The Lisbon Metropolitan Orchestra performs countless concerts in the city and surrounds, including free events in Palacio Foz.

Most of Lisbon's stage plays are comedies and revues – in Portuguese. The best-known theatre is the Teatro Nacional de Dona Maria II on Rossio (www.tndm.pt).

Cinemas tend to show foreign films in the original language with Portuguese subtitles. The renovated São Jorge picture house (www.cinemasaojorge.pt) on Avenida da Liberdade has three screens and is a major venue for film festivals. Large shopping centres such as Amoreiras or El Corte Inglés shelter multiplex cinemas.

Spectator sports

Lisbon is little different from other European cities in being mad about football. The city's two major teams are Benfica (www.slbenfica.pt), which plays at the Estádio da Luz, and Sporting Clube de Portugal (www.sporting.pt), which holds matches at Estádio José Alvade.

Bullfights take place in the Campo Pequeno Praça de Touros bullring (www.campopequeno.com) from Easter to October. Unlike Spanish bullfights the bull is not killed – at least not in the ring – but as barbed darts are planted in its upper back, it remains a bloody and cruel spectacle, and performances have become more controversial in recent years. At the end the bull is led away and is later slaughtered. A few bullfights are still held each year, but we do not recommend attendance.

Fado

Fado, the plaintive Portuguese musical genre – literally 'fate'– is based on a story or poem and accompanied by the Portuguese twelve-stringed *guitarra* or *viola* (acoustic Spanish guitar). Its roots can be traced back to the early 1820s and it has altered little since then. Lamentations of lost love, grief and destiny are all characteristic themes. Guitarists start off the proceedings with a warm-up number. The lights dim, the audience quietens, and a spotlight picks out a singer who begins to wail out a song of tragedy and despair. Their soulful voice sums up the Portuguese emotion, *saudade* – a swell of longing, regret and nostalgia. Sung by professionals, these chants are plangent, haunting and intensely moving, though to the unattuned ear they can sound strange and monotonous – hence the occasional jollification of traditional *fado* for the benefit of tourists. Most *fado* singers are women but you are also likely to hear a man perform the same sort of ballad with a strong, husky voice.

Benfica is one of Lisbon's major teams; the other is Sporting Clube de Portugal

Chronology

Fortunes have risen and fallen dramatically over the course of Lisbon's 3000-year history. Its great days are over, but in recent years the capital has flourished once again as a cosmopolitan city.

First settlers

c1200 BC The Phoenicians establish the trading post 'Alis Ubbo' ('Peaceful Harbour'), later changed to 'Olisipo', then to Lisbon.
205 BC Romans create Lusitania; Olisipo is made a municipality.
60 BC Julius Caesar makes Olisipo the western capital of Roman Empire.
AD 711 Moors from North Africa occupy Iberia.
1147 Afonso Henriques retakes Lisbon from the Moors and declares himself first King of Portugal.
1255 Capital of Portugal transferred from Coimbra to Lisbon.

Golden Age

1386 The Treaty of Windsor confirms England-Portugal Alliance, unbroken to this day. A year later King João I marries Philippa of Lancaster, daughter of John of Gaunt. Their third surviving son becomes 'Henry the Navigator'.
1415 Portuguese explorers reach Madeira, starting Age of Discoveries.
1425–1460 Period of exploration of the African coast by the Portuguese under Henry the Navigator; start of the slave trade.
1495–1521 King Manuel I on the throne; period of expansion and wealth.
1497–98 Vasco da Gama opens a sea route to India.
1500 Pedro Álvares Cabral lands in Brazil.
1543 Portuguese are the first Europeans to arrive in Japan.

Spanish and French rule

1568 King Sebastião invades Morocco, is killed and defeated.
1580 Portugal falls under Spanish rule for sixty years.
1640 End of Spanish rule. King João IV begins the Braganza dynasty.
1755 The Great Earthquake devastates Lisbon – and other parts of Portugal. The Marquês de Pombal takes charge of reconstruction.
1807–11 Invasions by Napoleonic troops at the start of the Peninsular War; the royal family flees the country to Brazil.
1821 The King returns from Brazil, handing rule back to the Braganzas under João VI.
1834 Prohibition of all religious orders, and church property seized and banned.

View of Lisbon and the River Tagus in the sixteenth century

Republic to dictatorship

1908 Popular revolution: assassination of King Carlos and Crown Prince in Lisbon.
1910 Republican uprising; the young King Manuel is deposed and given sanctuary by Britain, bringing to an end the Braganza dynasty.
1916 Germany declares war on Portugal.
1932 António de Oliveira Salazar becomes prime minister, effectively dictator.
1939–45 World War II. Portugal remains neutral on the outbreak of war.
1940 The Portuguese World Exhibition is held at Belém, emphasising the nation's independence.
1966 Opening of the Ponte de Salazar over the River Tejo, later renamed Ponte 25 de Abril in commemoration of the Carnation Revolution date.
1970 Death of Salazar.
1974 The peaceful 'Carnation Revolution' restores democracy; Portugal pulls out of African colonies and a million expatriates return.

Modern Lisbon

1986 Portugal joins the EU. Redevelopment of Lisbon.
1988 Fire destroys most of Lisbon's Chiado quarter.
1994 Lisbon voted European City of Culture.

Mascot for Expo 98, hosted in Lisbon

1998 Lisbon hosts Expo 98. Major building projects include the Ponte Vasco da Gama, Parque de Nações and the metro extension.
2002 The euro replaces the escudo as the national currency.
2004 Lisbon hosts the European Football Championship.
2007 EU leaders sign the Lisbon Treaty.
2011 Portuguese negotiate an economic bailout from the EU.
2016 Portugal wins the UEFA European Championship for the first time.
2020 Lisbon is European Green Capital 2020.
2025 Lisbon hosts EuroPride, highlighting its evolution as a prominent LGBTQ+ destination.

The 1755 Earthquake wrought terrible damage on the city

548
Coca-Cola

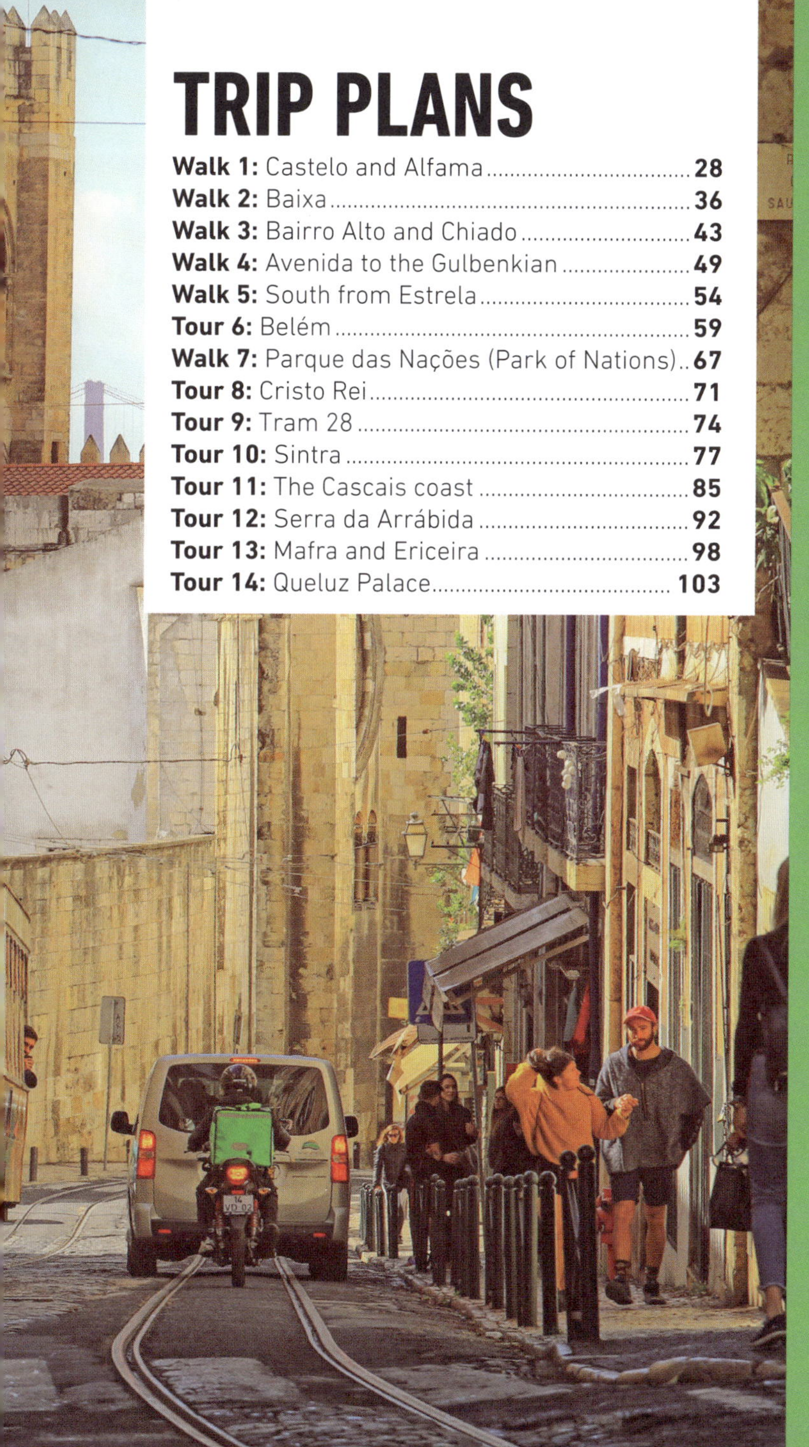

TRIP PLANS

WALK 1
Castelo and Alfama

Soak up the city's history in Lisbon's oldest, most picturesque and beguiling quarter. Enjoy sweeping panoramic views, meander through the tangle of alleys in the Alfama and end the day listening to the strains of bittersweet *fado*.

DISTANCE: 4km (2.5 miles)
TIME: A full day
START: Castelo de São Jorge
END: Alfama
POINTS TO NOTE: Save your stamina for steps and steep streets later and take the free lifts or public transport up to the castle. A lift operates 9am–9pm from Rua dos Fanqueiros 170 in Baixa. Cross the square diagonally for a second lift up to the Costa do Castelo, a short walk from the castle. Alternatively, take bus #737 from Praça da Figueira. Trams 12 and 28 trundle part of the way up to the castle but are usually packed with tourists. Pick up a plan when you buy your ticket for the castle – it can be tricky finding what's where. Allow a couple of hours. Aim to be in Alfama in the late afternoon and early evening when the small *tabernas* start to open and stay late to enjoy the *fado*. Watch your valuables in the alleys of Alfama. The flea market at Campo de Santa Clara is held on Tuesday and Saturday.

The name Alfama has a Moorish origin, named after the hot springs once found in this quarter. But the neighbourhood is much older, dating from the time of the Romans and even earlier settlers who first occupied the hillside. A section of the Roman amphitheatre, buried in the 1755 earthquake and excavated in 1964, can be seen near the cathedral. Under the Arabs and in the early years under Christian rule, this was the grandest part of the city.

Earthquakes, and most notably the great one in 1755, destroyed most of the fine buildings and the quarter was eventually abandoned to fishermen and the transient population. What survives is the labyrinthine layout of the Moors, as well as a remarkable village-like atmosphere. The whole area on the slope between the castle and the River Tagus is a jumble of steps and cobbled alleys, with flapping laundry and hidden gardens and patios.

Castelo de São Jorge

Crowning Lisbon's eastern hill is the imposing **Castelo de São Jorge ❶**

Castelo de São Jorge crowns the hill of ochre rooftops

(St George's Castle; www.castelodesaojorge.pt; charge). The castle ramparts can be seen from many city viewpoints, serving as an ever-present reminder of the capital's ancient roots.

As you enter the walled citadel you are stepping deep into the past. It was here that the foundations of Portugal were laid. In 1147 Portugal's first king, Afonso Henriques, launched a massive assault aided by rowdy crusaders, giant catapults and siege towers and conquered the castle, chasing the Moors from their citadel. The fall of Lisbon and the subsequent conquest of Moorish strongholds to the south ended five centuries of the Moors' presence in Portugal. The fortress became a home for royalty and the old Moorish buildings were modified and enlarged. In the sixteenth century the royal family moved to the Royal Ribeira Palace on Terreiro do Paço (Praça do Comércio) and the castle became a military garrison.

Earthquakes and wear and tear over the centuries have left little intact but there are fine views, archaeological remains and peaceful gardens with peacocks strutting around.

Within the citadel

Almost every hill in this elevated part of town has a *miradouro*, but the best panorama of all belongs to the castle. From the shaded belvedere, where Afonso stands, statue in hand, unfurls the many layers of Lisbon's storied history: from the Moorish quarter of Alfama below, westwards across to the seventeenth-century warren of the Bairro Alto and, between them, the tidy grid of the eighteenth-century Baixa streets built to the command of the Marquês de Pombal. Following the river, you can see as far as the twentieth-century Ponte 25 de Abril, and beyond the bridge on a clear day, the Monument to the Discoveries and Belém Tower, launching point of the great Portuguese voyages.

After absorbing the views from the belvedere, follow the flow through the gardens to what remains of the original Moorish palace. The **Núcleo Museológico** displays archaeological finds from the castle, set out in glass cabinets under brick vaults. Exhibits span 25 centuries, going back to the Iron Age, and are accompanied by excellent English-language labels on a variety of themes, including Arab foods, currency and tobacco ('the saintly herb', thought to heal migraines, grout and other illnesses). If it's time for coffee, take a break at the terraced café under the pines just beyond the museum.

Walk through the gardens and enter the castle via the so-called Tumbling Tower, today home to a **Camera Obscura** (guided tours every 15–20 minutes, in either Portuguese, Spanish or English – be sure to confirm before commencing), where real-time images of the city viewed through a periscope are projected onto a screen. A guide pinpoints

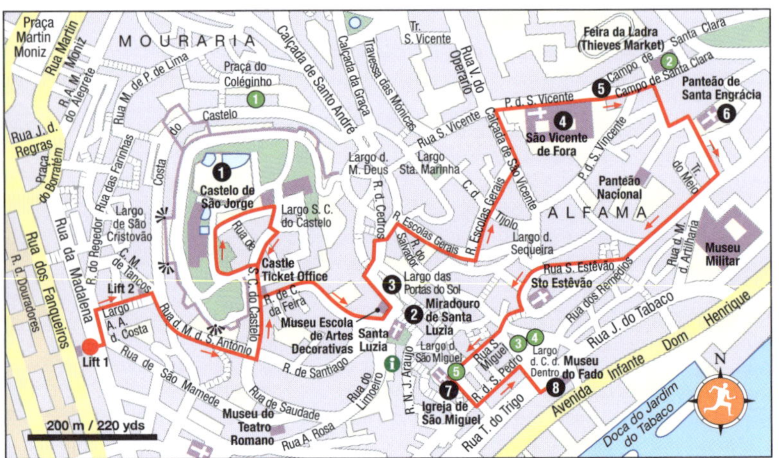

the main landmarks of Lisbon. Expect long queues in summer and no shows if it's dark and stormy.

Walk along the ramparts, climb up towers and, for the archaeological ruins, follow signs for the **Núcleo Arqueológico**. The site is divided into three parts: the seventh-century BC, the old Islamic quarter and the royal residence. Unless you take a guided tour (free) you may be not much the wiser, but it's a peaceful site shaded beneath umbrella pines and there are lovely views across the Alfama.

There is no café within the walls of the castle and most options nearby are rather touristy. **Café da Garagem**, see 1, with its wide windows, is just a short walk away. Alternatively, have lunch later in the Alfama.

Santa Cruz quarter

Exit the castle and explore the atmospheric narrow alleys of the **Santa Cruz quarter** by turning left along the Rua de Santa Cruz do Castelo, then right at the square, following the Rua do Recolhimento. You may well be tempted to take a break at one of the pretty cafés or little seafood-serving *tascas* spilling out onto open-air patios. Back at the castle, turn left and follow the crowds down to the **Largo do Contador Mor**, with its shady restaurants offering grilled sardines and sangria.

Miradouro de Santa Luzia

Continue downhill, along the Travessa de Santa Luzia, for the romantic **Miradouro de Santa Luzia** 2. This small balustraded garden, with great

On the castle's ramparts

swathes of bougainvillea and a vine-clad pergola, has stunning views over the sea of rooftops that cascade down to the Tagus and there's usually a busker playing. Two detailed and dramatic panels of *azulejos* on the church wall show Lisbon's waterfront as it was before the Great Earthquake, including the royal palace on the Terreiro do Paço. Told in tiles, too, is the story of Martim Moniz, close friend of Afonso Henriques: in the 1147 assault on São Jorge castle, he is said to have seen the Moors closing the castle doors and sacrificed himself by holding open a castle gateway as Moors hacked him to death. The heroic act gave the Christian soldiers time to secure the entryway, and eventually capture the castle.

Largo das Portas do Sol

Just up the street is another magnificent *miradouro* at **Largo das Portas do Sol** ❸. The area is vibrant with life and colour as vintage trams and tuk-tuks rattle by and tourists throng on the belvedere to take snapshots of the Alfama unfolding below. Presiding over the square is a statue of St Vincent, patron saint of Lisbon.

Across the road, the fine seventeenth-century Azurara Palace has been filled with magnificent pieces of furniture, Chinese porcelain, a priceless silver collection and several tapestries from sixteenth- to nineteenth-century Portugal and its colonies, forming the **Museu de Artes Decorativas Portuguesas** (Museum of Portuguese Decorative Arts; www.fress.pt; charge). The museum belongs to the Ricardo do Espírito Santo Silva Foundation, which was established in the 1950s by the eponymous banker who bought the palace to house his valuable collection. The foundation has eighteen workshops where artisans practice traditional crafts such as woodcarving, metalwork, gilding and bookbinding.

São Vicente de Fora

On the eastern heights beyond the dense quarters of the Alfama, and clearly visible from Largo Portas do Sol, are two remarkable churches. To reach the vast **Igreja e Mosteiro de São Vicente de Fora** ❹ (Church and Monastery of St Vincent Beyond the Walls; www.mosteirodesaovicentedefora.com; monastery charge, church free), either hop on Tram No 28 or follow the tram lines north, taking the right-hand fork down the hill to the narrowing and winding Rua das Escolas Gerais. Where the line starts to ascend and divides into two again, the church looms large to your right, its Mannerist facade ornamented with animated statues. *De fora*, meaning outside, reflects the fact that the church once stood beyond the city walls. Founded by Afonso Henriques, after retaking the city from the Moors, the church was reconstructed in the late sixteenth century around the time of the Inquisition.

Museu de Artes Decorativas

The imposing castle walls

Santo António

On the night of 12 June, the eve of the festival of Santo António, the city pays homage to its revered native son with a cheerfully noisy parade down the Avenida da Liberade, followed by celebrations in Alfama. Streets are strung with bunting, colourful lights illuminate squares and alleys, sardines are grilled by the thousand, wine flows, music plays, people dance – and buy or sell pots of basil for luck. All are welcome. On the nights of São Joao (23 June) and São Pedro (28th), it's almost as festive. Just downhill from Lisbon's cathedral is the little Igreja de Sant António, built in 1812 to honour the saint. Known to the rest of the world as St Antony of Padua, to Lisboetas he is Santo António di Lisboa. The crypt, all that survived the 1755 earthquake, was built on the spot where the saint's house stood, according to local lore. St Anthony is invoked as the patron saint of lost things, and locals also appeal to him for help in finding a spouse; sometimes bridal bouquets are left at his altar in the cathedral, along with thanks for all his good work.

Monastery

The entrance to the monastery is to the left as you leave the church. Built over an enormous cistern, which you see near the entrance, many of the monastery's walls and its cloisters are sumptuously lined with ornate and patriotic *azulejos*. Between the two cloisters is the exuberantly decorated sacristy, below which, it is said, lie the tombs of the Teutonic knights who helped Afonso in the Lisbon conquest. On the upper floor, in the museum area, don't miss the glazed tiled panels of the much-loved **Fables of La Fontaine**, depicted in 38 tableaux. The former refectory serves as the Royal Pantheon of the Braganza family, the last dynasty to rule Portugal. Tombs of royalty include Catherine of Braganza, queen to Charles II of England, Carlos I and his heir Prince Luís Felipe, assassinated together in 1908, and Manuel II who went into exile in Twickenham, southwest London, where his mother had been born, when the Portuguese monarchy was overthrown in 1910.

Campo de Santa Clara and the Panteão Nacional

Duck down the alley to the left of the church for the **Campo de Santa Clara** ❺. On Tuesday and Saturday all peace and tranquillity leaves the square with the colourful **Feira da Ladra** (Thieves' Market). It's worth browsing through the splendid selection of junk for the occasional gem. Fans of fungi should make note of the wonderful mushroom restaurant, **Santa Clara dos Cogumelos**, see ②, although it's only open for dinner apart from at weekends.

From the square, follow the brown signs for another pantheon, the

Looking to the Igreja e Mosteiro de São Vicente de Fora

vast **Panteão de Santa Engrácia** ❻ (National Pantheon; www.panteaonacional.gov.pt; charge), just downhill from the monastery. This grandiosely domed Baroque building was begun in the 1682 but took nearly three hundred years to complete, hence the Portuguese saying for a task never done: *'obras de Santa Engrácia'*. The church honours great figures in Portuguese history such as Vasco da Gama and Henry the Navigator; from more recent history are the real tombs of presidents of the Republic and contributors to Portuguese culture, including the famous *fado* singer Amália Rodrigues (1920–1999; which always has fresh flowers) and well-known footballers. A lift (often with queues, but you can also climb up) affords a wonderful panorama of the city.

Sé Patriarcal

On the western fringes of the Alfama is Lisbon's twelfth-century **Sé** (Cathedral; www.sedelisboa.pt; charge), founded on the site of a mosque. The church has been heavily restored but retains its solid Romanesque facade with twin castellated towers, softened by a rose window. The peaceful thirteenth-century cloisters have been excavated to reveal signs of Iron Age, Roman and Moorish occupation. The treasury houses relics associated with patron saint São Vicente. Legend has it that these were transported to Lisbon from Cape St Vincent in southern Portugal in a boat guarded by two sacred black ravens – the symbol of the city.

Heart of the Alfama

From the pantheon square drop down into the picturesque heart of the Alfama by taking the Rua dos Remédios then swerve right along Rua do Vigário for the **Igreja de Santo Estêvão**. Here you'll find yet another *miradouro*, with views of the river over tumbling rooftops and small gardens. Take the narrow and steep stairway Beco do Carneiro, on the far side of the church, and cross the street for the slender Rua São Miguel, with its little shops and tiny alleys and stairways shooting off. (Or you can avoid the Beco and walk via the airier Calçadinha de Santo Estêvão and Rua da Regueira.)

This brings you to the **Igreja de São Miguel** ❼ (usually closed) which dates back to the twelfth century but, like so many of Lisbon's churches, was rebuilt after the Great Earthquake of 1755. If you're in the area in June, when Alfama celebrates the festas of the popular saints – for virtually the whole month – the neighbourhood is festooned with decorations and explodes with music (see box).

South of the church, turn left onto Alfama's main shopping street, the cobbled **Rua de São Pedro da Praça**. This used to be the site of a lively fish market with a cacophony of shouting

Flea market wares at the Feira da Ladra

Azulejos museum

Although out on a limb from the centre of Lisbon, it's well worth making the effort to visit the Museu Nacional do Azulejo (National Tile Museum; Rua da Madre de Deus 4; bus #794; www.museudoazulejo.gov.pt; charge). Set in the magnificent Manueline Madre de Deus convent, the museum is devoted to this notable Portuguese art form. It was founded in 1509 by Queen Dona Leonor, widow of King João II. Displays in the two-storey cloister chart the development of the *azulejo*, from the early Moorish origins in the fifteenth century through Spanish influence and the creation of Portugal's own *azulejos*. Thousands of tiles over the centuries show gradual changes in colour, style and taste and include seventeenth-century hunting scenes, narrative eighteenth-century panels, Art Deco flourishes and tiles right up to the late twentieth century, where the art form found new expression in major projects such as the metro.

The eighteenth-century Igreja da Madre de Deus is a heady mix of Rococo gilt, frescoes and *azulejos*. Side walls are adorned with tiles from The Netherlands; those in the sacristy were made in Lisbon's Rato factory. Don't miss the Lisbon Panorama, a 23m (75ft) -long expanse of 1300 *azulejos* that records the riverside as it looked before the 1755 earthquake.

fishmongers and families gathering for meals in the street. Many moved out to quarters with better living conditions and nowadays, immigrants and younger residents have moved in. This is the main shopping street, lined with dinky old-fashioned groceries, family-run *tascas*, *casas de fado* and hole-in-the-wall bars offering cheap shots of port or *ginjinha*. With the new generation and influx of tourism there is also a growing crop of modern shops and bars springing up in newly restored buildings.

The Rua de São Pedro da Praça leads to the busy **Largo do Chafariz de Dentro**, named after the seventeenth-century fountain *(chafariz)*, originally within *(dentro)* the city walls. For a meal you could opt for unfussy **O Cartaxeiro**, see ③, a people-watching gem on the square, or explore the atmospheric alleyways and choose from cheap and characteristic eateries, with fresh sardines, paper tablecloths and bills scribbled on scraps of paper.

Museu do Fado

At the southern gateway to the Alfama, within a revamped building which was Lisbon's first pumphouse, is the **Museu do Fado** ❽ (Fado Museum; Largo do Chafariz de Dentro 1; www.museudofado.pt; charge). The museum sets the tone for the soul of the district, paying homage to Lisbon's traditional form of song and its creators. Donations from the performers and their families enabled

There is an incredible collection of vernacular tiles at Museu Nacional do Azulejo

Food and drink

1 Café da Garagem
Costa do Castelo 75;
www.teatrodagaragem.com; €
This theatre's café is a great spot for a coffee and cake, light lunch or to hear jazz concerts in the evening. Tables are arranged strategically in the long and narrow space, overlooking the wide windows that perfectly frame Lisbon's jumble of houses below. Arrive early to snag a front-row seat or one outside; the exterior terrace is tiny.

2 Santa Clara dos Cogumelos
Campo de Santa Clara 7;
www.santaclaradoscogumelos.com;
€€
A temple to mushrooms, this Italian-run restaurant feature fungi in *petiscos* (tapas), main courses and even desserts. Try organic shitake with coriander or mushroom ravioli with black trumpet sauce and end with porcini ice cream.

3 O Cartaxeiro
Largo do Chafariz de Dentro 23; tel: 218 881 215; €€
Watch the comings and goings from the edge of the square as you tuck into one of the *pratos do dia* scribbled on the chalkboard, ranging from grilled fish to house speciality *arroz de pato* (duck rice), so popular it always sells out before the end of service.

4 Parreirinha de Alfama
Beco do Espírito Santo 1;
www.parreirinhadealfama.com; €€€€
Just off Largo do Chafariz de Dentro in Alfama, this one of Lisbon's oldest and most famous *fado* houses, popular with locals as well as tourists, though more for the music than its food.

5 A Baîuca
Rua de São Miguel 20;
www.instagram.com/abaiuca_; €€€
A small, characteristic *fado* venue in the heart of the Alfama opposite the Church of São Miguel. Dinner is compulsory, with minimum spend.

the opening of the centre in 1998. Pick up an audio guide (free with admission) to listen to bygone stars – or hear them in a mock *fado* tavern.

If inspired by *fado*, while away the early part of the evening in one of the local bars, then dine in a *casa de fado*. Just off Largo do Chafariz de Dentro is the well-known **Parreirinha de Alfama**, see 4, or near the Church of Sao Miguel is **A Baîuca**, see 5, a more low-key affair with amateur *fado*. A third option is **Clube de Fado** (Rua de São João da Praça 92; www.clubedefado.pt), hosting well-known *fado* singers in the bar and restaurant.

Narrow alleys and crumbling facades in Alfama

WALK 2
Baixa

Spend an unhurried couple of hours strolling through the heart of the city with its bustling streets and squares, alfresco cafés and old-world stores. From the waterfront this walk heads north to lively Rossio and ends at the Elevador de Santa Justa for fine views of the capital.

DISTANCE: 2km (1.25 miles)
TIME: 2 hours plus, depending on visits
START: Praça do Comércio
END: Elevador de Santa Justa
POINTS TO NOTE: Walk 3 could easily follow on from this route if you took the Elevador da Glória from Praça dos Restauradores at the end of the itinerary, rather than the Elevador de Santa Justa.

The Baixa has always been the commercial hub of the city, but before the Great Earthquake of 1755 it was a warren of alleys between the capital's two main squares. The earthquake and ensuing tidal wave and fire devastated the area, and it was from the ruins that the Marquês de Pombal, chief minister of King José I, rebuilt a new city of uniform buildings on a grid street plan.

The fact that this was always a quarter of trade is reflected in the names of the streets: Rua dos Sapateiros for the shoemakers, Rua da Prata for silversmiths, Rua Áurea (also called Rua do Ouro) for goldsmiths and Rua dos Fanqueiros for haberdashers. A few of these crafts still exist.

Praça do Comércio

The Marquês de Pombal designed the monumental **Praça do Comércio ❶** (Commerce Square) as the centrepiece of his post-earthquake reconstruction. The square lies directly on the harbour, with marble steps leading down to the River Tagus. The Cais das Colunas (Columns' Pier) was for centuries the main entrance to the city. Nowadays, this is a popular spot for buskers or tourists who sit on the steps and take in the river views.

Lisboetas call the square by its old name, the Terreiro do Paço (Palace Square), after the Royal Ribeira Palace that was built here by Manuel I in 1510, but which was wiped out by the earthquake. The then-reigning monarch, José I, chose to move to the more stable parish of Ajuda, which later became part of Belém. An equestrian statue of the king takes centre stage

Praça do Comércio, Lisbon's impressive waterfront square

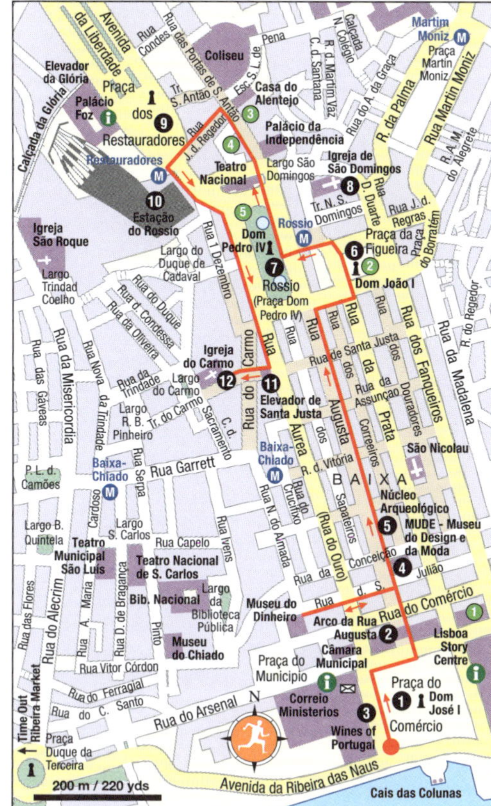

were riding in an open landau with the king's wife and younger son Manuel. Their assassins were shot on the spot. The first Portuguese regicide in centuries forced the young and unprepared Manuel to the throne. He would be Portugal's last king.

Arco da Rua Augusta

Stately arcades and government buildings flank three sides of the vast square. On the north side the **Arco da Rua Augusta** ❷ (also known as the Arco da Vitória) is a triumphal arch crowned by a female allegory of Glory, holding laurel wreaths above Genius and Bravery. Heroic statues below (from left to right) represent Viriatus, the Lusitanian warrior who died resisting Roman

in the square, his horse trampling on snakes (symbols of evil) and the elephant representing Portugal's African and Indian colonies. A later monarch, King Carlos I and his heir, Luís Felipe, were shot in this square in 1908 as they

expansion; Nuno Álvares Pereira, whose victory over Castilian forces ensured the nation's independence; Vasco da Gama; and the Marquês de Pombal. The two recumbent figures represent the rivers Tagus and Douro. An elevator

Riverside promenade

On the west side of the Praça do Comércio, the waterfront Ribeiras das Naus has been transformed into a pleasant, tree-lined promenade that has the feel of the seaside (there are even patches of sand). Open and spacious, it's popular with joggers, cyclists, strollers and sunbathers. The promenade leads to Cais do Sodré, a ferry terminal, station and former red-light district that has been fully revamped. Apart from clubs, live-music venues and bars, it is also home to the Mercado da Ribeira, the old domed market opposite the station that now has a wonderful food court, Time Out Market Lisbon, with gourmet kiosks open all day and evening (see page 117). Since opening in 2014, it has rapidly become one of the capital's top tourist attractions – no mean feat in a city as packed with points of interest as Lisbon.

and steps lead up to the roof for views of the Baixa and the Tagus (charge).

To absorb life on the square, choose one of the people-watching cafés, the most famous of which is the **Café Martinho da Arcada**, see ①, east of the Arco da Rua Augusta. If it is after noon you could sample regional wines at the **Wines of Portugal** ❸ (www.winesofportugal.com), a tasting room located beneath the arches on the west side of the square. Purchase a chip card (minimum charge), take a glass and help yourself to 5cl shots from the taps. There is English labelling for each wine and friendly, helpful staff. You can also join a guided session and bone up on the diversity of varietals from different Portuguese regions.

Across the square and within the tourist office building is the **Lisboa Story Centre** (www.lisboastorycentre.pt; charge), an informative if underwhelming interactive centre that takes visitors through Lisbon's major historical events from the foundation of the city to the modern day. The AskMe Lisboa office here provides free maps and abundant leaflets on tourist attractions (there's also another office across the square).

The triumphal arch leads into pedestrianised Rua Augusta, the lively main thoroughfare pressing north to Rossio. On the right is **MUDE – Museu do Design e da Moda** ❹ (www.mude.pt; charge), a collection of twentieth-century design and fashion, housed within a starkly converted bank building. The vault and second-floor gallery are devoted to temporary exhibitions. However, it's arguably one of Lisbon's least interesting museums.

A short detour left along Rua de São Julião will bring you to the Largo de São Julião, site of the Museo do Dinheiro (Money Museum; www.museudodinheiro.pt; free). At a cost of 34

Ribeiras das Naus life

million euros, the Bank of Portugal rebuilt the Baroque Church of São Julião, previously used as the bank's vault. During excavations here in 2010 the thirteenth-century Wall of King Dinis was discovered in the crypt of the former church and is now on display behind glass. The main museum traces the evolution of money in Portugal and around the world, with highly innovative and interactive displays. Visitors, for example, are invited to mint a coin or touch a 12kg (26lb) gold bar.

From Rua Augusta, turn right onto **Rua da Conceição**, a street traditionally known for its tiny, but sadly fast-disappearing, haberdasheries. The lovely little Retrosaria Bijou at No 91 is a fine example. Take the next left for the fascinating **Núcleo Arqueológico** ❺ (Rua dos Correeiros 21; www.fundacaomillenniumbcp.pt; prebook free guided tours), hidden below (and managed by) the HQ of Millennium BCP, Portugal's biggest privately owned bank. An archaeological dig in the 1990s revealed layers of ruins covering 2500 years of history, and in particular the remains of a fish-processing centre that was located on the river in Roman times. Sauces and condiments were made from leftovers of fish, molluscs and oysters, soaked in salt and aromatic herbs. The mixture was heated to accelerate decomposition and then left to mature.

Continue along Rua dos Correeiros, where restaurants serving Portuguese fish dishes may well tempt you. The street is more old-fashioned and less touristy than Rua Augusta, though not without its bar touts. Turn left at Rua da Vitória (with views of the Elevador de Santa Justa at the end of the street) and return to Rua Augusta for a spot of retail therapy and entertainment from frozen statues. At the top of the street, swerve right for **Praça da Figueira** ❻. Formerly the city's main marketplace, it is now a traffic-encircled square that could be bypassed were it not the location of one of the most famous patisseries in the city: the **Confeitaria Nacional**, see ②. The equestrian statue of King João I, high on a pedestal in the centre of the square, was erected in 1971. With the king on your right, walk along the west side of the square, turning left for Rossio.

Rossio

The square popularly called **Rossio** ❼ is officially the Praça Dom Pedro IV, named after the king whose statue tops a pillar in the middle. This is the true core of Lisbon, a large busy square and meeting place, with fountains and florists, shoe shiners and pavement cafés. The great open space was once the site of bullfights, carnivals, public executions, burning of Inquisition victims and other public events. The palace that served as the headquarters for the Inquisitor-General formerly dominated the north edge, but since the 1840s has been

Arco da Rua Augusta

Walking on art

Portugal is renowned for its *azulejos* (see page 46) but another striking aspect of Portuguese identity is the *calçada portuguesa* or Portuguese paving. Everywhere you walk in Lisbon you will spot attractively decorated streets and squares. Tiny blocks of white limestone and black basalt are painstakingly cut and laid by hand to create patterns or images, similar to a mosaic. Many of the finest examples of these cobblestone designs can be seen along Avenida da Liberdade. The tradition was inspired by Roman mosaics, but today's patterned pavements in the city date to the mid-nineteenth century, following completion of the wave design, known as the 'Largo Mar' (Wide Sea) in Rossio, honouring the Portuguese discoveries. You can still occasionally see pavers (*calceteiros*) repairing the streets, but the maintenance work is costly, the mosaics can be slippery, and the number of craftspeople is dwindling. It may not be long before these fine mosaics are replaced with something more modern and practical.

occupied by the **Teatro Nacional Dona Maria II** (www.tndm.pt; guided tours Monday only, charge).

The most famous café on the square is the elegantly fronted Art Nouveau **Café Nicola**, a former haunt of artists, politicians and intellectuals. The equally famed *Pastelaria Suiça* has now relocated to the neighbouring square, Praça da Figueira. Both are good for watching the world go by, though you pay for the privilege and are often pestered by peddlers.

If you spot locals or tourists gathering around hole-in-the-wall bars in and around the Largo São Domingos, northwest of Rossio, they will be quaffing shots of *ginjinha*, a sweet cherry liqueur that comes with *(com elas)* or without *(sem elas)* the cherries. Two of the best-known are **A Ginjinha** on the square and the nearby **Ginjinha Sem Rival** at Rua Das Portas de Santo Antão 7. The tipple is not to everyone's taste but it's cheap and worth a try; ask for it in a chocolate cup for something sweeter.

Igreja de São Domingos

The burnt, cave-like interior of the Dominican **Igreja de São Domingos** ❽ (Largo de São Domingos; www.patriarcado-lisboa.pt; free) is an evocative reminder of the city's natural disasters: the earthquakes of 1531 and 1755, the fires following the latter, and another more recent fire in 1959. The walls and altar are charred, the pilasters blackened and battered. This is one of the city's most-loved churches, with a steady stream of worshippers.

The cobbled and pedestrianised **Rua das Portas de Sant Antão** running north is flanked by restaurants with

Teatro Nacional Dona Maria II

touting waiters and more *ginjinha* bars. If you fancy fine dining your best bet is **Gambrinus**, see 3, at No 23–25. For more affordable, filling fare try **Casa do Alentejo**, see 4, at No 58. Inside you'll find a riot of interior styling: Moorish courtyards, Art Deco flourishes, a grand banquet hall and a restaurant decorated with panels of *azulejos*. If you simply want to sample a few Alentejo specialities, there is an outlet next door with wines, cheeses and smoked sausage.

Praça dos Restauradores

Across the road, take the Rua do Jardim do Regardor which brings you into the monumental **Praça dos Restauradores** 9. The obelisk here celebrates the overthrow of Spanish rule in 1640. The square stretches to the broad, elegant Avenida da Liberdade, which runs for nearly a mile, and is famous for its smart designer shops (see Walk 4). Palacio Foz, the pink palace on the west side of the square, houses a useful tourist office and hosts occasional concerts. Beside it, the lovely Art Deco erstwhile Teatro Eden is now the *Eden Aparthotel*, with a cluster of tourist apartments and a rooftop swimming pool. On the south side of the square is the five-star *Hotel Avenida Palace* and, beyond, the splendid mock-Manueline **Estação do Rossio** 10 (Rossio Station) framed by palatial Moorish horseshoe arches. From here frequent trains run to Sintra. There are fine views of the castle from the station terrace, accessed via two sets of escalators. Across the road from the station, atop *Hotel Altis*, is the **Rossio Gastrobar**, see 5, a swanky dining room with excellent views.

Elevador de Santa Justa

Take the Rua Áurea south from Rossio, then turn right along the Rua de Santa Justa to see one of the most bizarre and intriguing structures in the city: the neo-Gothic **Elevador de Santa Justa** 11 (www.carris.pt; charge), a wrought-iron lift built by Raul Mésnier, an apprentice of Gustave Eiffel. Be prepared for long queues, even off season. The lift is part of Lisbon's public transport system so you can use an all-day bus/metro ticket or a Viva Viagem card and trundle up and down at will. Alternatively, you can walk up the steps – as the locals do.

The *elevador* was inaugurated in 1901, the year electric trams began a transport service on the hilly, winding streets. The ascent in two wood-panelled cabins of the 45m (147ft) -high lift is swift but at the top you can climb a spiral staircase to the *miradouro* (extra charge) for great views of the city.

A walkway links the lift to the lovely Largo do Carmo in Bairro Alto. End the day amid the Gothic ruins of the **Igreja do Carmo** 12 (Carmelite Church, see page 46), a moving reminder of the devastation wrought by the earthquake of 1755.

Estação do Rossio

Elevador de Santa Justa's unique structure

Food and drink

❶ Café Martinho da Arcada

Praça do Comércio 3;
www.martinhodaarcada.pt; €€
One of Lisbon's oldest cafés, dating from 1782, this charming haunt is renowned as a former hangout of literati including the great Portuguese poet, Fernando Pessoa (1888–1935). Photographs of Pessoa and his favourite table have been preserved for posterity. Stop by for a cup of coffee, ideally with a couple of *pastéis de nata* (custard tarts). Full meals also available. Pavement tables have views (and fumes) of trams rattling by.

❷ Confeitaria Nacional

Praça da Figueira 18B;
www.confeitarianacional.com; €
One of the oldest and best confectioners in town, *Confeitaria Nacional* has been in the same family for six generations. The array of pastries is a feast for the eyes – as is the elegant French-style interior. The speciality is *'Bolo-Rei'* made to the original secret recipe, brought from France in 1850. Light lunches are also available.

❸ Gambrinus

Rua das Portas de Santo Antão 23;
www.gambrinuslisboa.com; €€€€
One of the city's most famous restaurants, *Gambrinus* has a club-like atmosphere, top-notch traditional service, fabulous fresh fish as well as meat specialities such as partridge pie. The favourite dessert is *crêpes suzette*.

❹ Casa do Alentejo

Rua das Portas de Santo Antão 58;
https://casadoalentejo.pt; €€
Once a palace belonging to the Viscounts of Alverca, since the 1920s the *casa* has been the cultural and social centre of Alentejanos (residents of the Alentejo region) living in Lisbon. Its traditional restaurant serves excellent, well-priced and hearty Alentejo dishes for lunch and dinner. Typical dishes are *açorda* (bread and garlic soup), lamb casserole, oven-baked rabbit, and regional desserts. Alternatively, opt for tapas in the simple *taberna* with a little courtyard.

❺ Rossio Gastrobar

Rua 1 de Dezembro 105;
tel: 213 426 195; €€€
With some of the best views across Lisbon, this rooftop restaurant is a real treat – even if you only drop by for a cocktail. Dishes range from small sharing plates, such as the finest cuts of acorn-fed Iberian ham, to Portuguese comforting classics with a twist, including shellfish and seaweed rice or *pica pau* (beef in gravy).

The ruins of Igreja do Carmo

WALK 3
Bairro Alto and Chiado

Lose yourself in the warren of the Bairro Alto, shop in the chic Chiado, then dine out, listen to *fado* or join the bar-hopping revellers. The Bairro Alto boasts the coolest nightlife scene in the city.

DISTANCE: 3.5km (2 miles)
TIME: An afternoon, minimum two hours
START: Elevador da Glória
END: Bairro Alto
POINTS TO NOTE: Bairro Alto is served by the metro Baixa-Chiado (blue and green lines), Tram 28 and various buses. Arrive in the afternoon and stay the evening to sample the excellent restaurants and lively nightlife. Advance reservations are essential for *Belcanto* restaurant.

High above the Baixa, the maze-like Bairro Alto (Upper Town) is a hilly and dense quarter, full of picturesque peeling houses lining cobbled, car-free streets. Formerly run-down and sleazy, it is today an area of family-run *tascas* (restaurants), quirky, arty shops and bohemian boutiques. But more than anywhere in Lisbon, the Bairro Alto leads a double life. Sleepy by day, it becomes the capital's nightlife epicentre after dark. Very different in feel is neighbouring Chiado, long renowned for dispensing Lisbon's most elegant goods – silverware, leather, fashion and books – along with fine pastries and teashops. It was once a haunt of the literati, many of whom frequented its famous *A Brasiliera* café.

Miradouro and Convent of São Pedro de Alcântara

From Praça dos Restauradores, take the **Elevador da Glória** ❶, the picturesque yellow funicular that has plied the Rua da Glória since circa 1900. (You may have to queue – locals tend to walk up the hill rather than wait). At the top admire the expansive views across Baixa from the belvedere of the **Miradouro de São Pedro de Alcântara** ❷. All the distinctive buildings are flagged on a large pictorial tiled table. The view takes in a great sweep of the Lisbon skyline from the Sé (cathedral) and castle ramparts to the contemporary skyscrapers in the north. Nab one of the benches in the belvedere gardens or an outdoor deckchair at the café at the far end. Look out for the fountain and monument dedicated to the newspaper

Elevador da Glória makes light work of the hill

magnate, Eduardo Coelho, with the statue of a newspaper delivery boy below.

Across the road from the gardens is the **Convento de São Pedro de Alcântara** ❸ (Rua Luísa Todi 1; www.agendalx.pt; charge for convent, church and chapel free). The highlights here are the glorious blue-and-white *azulejos* depicting *Scenes from the Life of St Peter of Alcântara* on the lower level of the church, the *trompe l'oeil* ceiling and the funerary chapel of Cardinal Veríssimo de Lancastre with glorious inlaid marble.

Igreja de San Roque

Continue down the street for **Largo Trindade Coelho** ❹, with its statue of a lottery seller and a kiosk selling the real thing. A more recent sculpture in the square is that of Lisbon-born António Viera (1608–1697), a Jesuit priest, diplomat and missionary, who lived in Brazil from the age of 6 years. He is depicted with three Indian children from Brazil, whom he converted to Christianity. Overlooking the square is the Jesuit **Igreja de São Roque** ❺ (Church of St Roch; www.museusaoroque.scml.pt; charge). The dull facade, rebuilt after the 1755 earthquake, belies a lavishly decorated interior. The beautiful *trompe l'oeil* dates from 1589 and is the only surviving example in Lisbon of a Mannerist-style ceiling. Of the eight richly decorated chapels, the most opulent is that of St John the Baptist, fourth on the left, incorporating lapis lazuli, agate, porphyry, alabaster, amethyst, jade and different marbles. King João V, Lisbon's most extravagant

Rich detail at Igreja de San Roque

king, ordered the altar from Rome, where teams of artists and artisans worked on it for five years. The chapel was blessed by Pope Benedict X1V before being dismantled and carried in three ships to Lisbon where it was permanently installed in 1747. Either side of the chancel are two reliquary altars, containing relics of Holy Martyrs (men on the left side, women on the right), dating from the sixteenth century onwards.

Adjoining the church is the **Museu de São Roque**, with a beautifully presented collection of precious reliquaries, paintings, delicate jewellery and eighteenth-century textiles.

Streets and squares of Bairro Alto

Most of the Bairro Alto's restaurants and bars are hidden in the knot of streets to the west of the Rua de São Pedro de Alcântara and this is the place to return later for a meal and a taste of the neighbourhood's nightlife. For a daylight impression of the narrow lanes with their wrought-iron balconies, flapping laundry, street art and graffiti, take a walk from the square along the **Travessa da Queimada**. Explore the neat grid of streets, then press south along the **Rua do Norte**, past the *fado* bars and down to **Praça Luís de Camões** ❻. If you hear a bell ringing, make for **Manteigaria**, a patisserie just off the square at Rua do Loreto 2 – it signals a fresh batch of oven-warm, mouthwatering *pastéis de nata* (custard tarts).

The Praça Luís de Camões is dominated by the imposing statue of the eponymous poet, with nine literary figures on pedestals below. Another cultural idol lies close by in the Rua do Alecrim, beyond the square. A statue of the nineteenth-century novelist, Eça de Queiróz (1845–1900), gazes upon a scantily veiled muse in the Largo do Barão Quintela. Overlooking the square on Rua do Alecrim is the beautifully restored **Palácio Chiado**, see ❶, one of the city's fine gastronomic venues.

Jardim Botânico

For a cool, shady spot you may want to deviate north of the Miradouro, around ten minutes' walk up the main Rua de São Pedro de Alcântara, for the **Jardim Botânico** (Botanical Garden; Rua da Escola Politécnica 58; www.ulisboa.pt; charge). The walk takes you via the Principe Real quarter with its lovely gardens, antique shops and hip stores. The Jardim Botânico is reached through the university gate alongside the Academy of Sciences. Founded in 1873, this is primarily an arboretum with large, shady trees, ferns and palms. Don't go expecting immaculate flowerbeds.

Museu de São Roque

Azulejos

Azulejos, the hand-painted, glazed tiles omnipresent in Lisbon, are the Moors' most lasting legacy. Lining church walls, embellishing palaces and humble houses, gracing gardens and fonts, these ceramic tiles are a delight. The tiled panels are not merely decorative. Following the Great Earthquake in 1755, fires devastated much of Lisbon and the surrounding area and *azulejos* were widely used to protect buildings from going up in flames again. At the Museu Nacional do Azulejo (see page 34), which has a magnificent and comprehensive collection of Portuguese tiles, you can see how they are made.

Chiado

Retrace your steps, turning right at the top of the street for the **Largo do Chiado** ❼, overlooked by two Baroque churches. Head left into the Rua Nova da Trindade where you'll see the Teatro da Trinidade, whose heyday was the 1930s and 40s though it continues to host plays and opera. Turn right for the Largo Rafael Bordalo Pinheiro, with cafés, restaurants and the nineteenth-century Casa do Ferreira das Tabuletas with *trompe l'oeil azulejos* of allegorical figures representing Earth, Water, Commerce, Industry, Science and Agriculture. Continue down Rua da Trindade for the Largo do Carmo.

Igrejo do Carmo

The lovely **Largo do Carmo**, with its tree-shaded cafés and fountain, is overlooked by the former **Convento do Carmo**, HQ of the Paramilitary National Republican Guard where the prime minister and conservative leaders took refuge as crowds thronged outside during the 1974 Revolution. To the right is the entrance to the **Igreja do Carmo** ❽ and **Museo Arqueológico del Carmo** (www.museuarqueologicodocarmo.pt; charge).

On All Saints' Day in 1755, when the Great Earthquake struck (see page 11), the church roof fell on a full congregation. It has stood in ruins ever since, a mere shell but a highly evocative reminder of the catastrophic event. The roofless Gothic arches silhouetted against the blue sky is one of Lisbon's most striking sights. The Carmelite church was founded in the fourteenth century and when it was built, it was the largest church in Lisbon. The eclectic museum in the chancel has exhibits ranging from a Roman tomb to Spanish-Moorish *azulejos* and mummified remains from Peru.

Rua Garrett

Take the narrow Calçada do Sacramento, which drops down from the Largo do Carmo into **Rua Garrett** ❾. In 1988 this fashionable shopping street of the Chiado was devastated by a fire which started in nearby Rua

Facade of Convento do Carmo

do Carmo. Many of the eighteenth-century buildings were destroyed, along with shops and offices. The fire wiped out two of Europe's oldest department stores, including the legendary Amarzéns do Chiado. Portugal's internationally renowned architect, Álvaro Siza, oversaw the tasteful reconstruction of the neighbourhood, especially along the Rua do Carmo.

Turn left and you will find the rebuilt Armazéns do Chiado shopping centre, and just down the Rua do Carmo on the left, **Santini**, with irresistible ice creams. Head west along Rua Garrett, passing elegant Art Nouveau shop fronts, to **A Brasileira**, see ②, where a bronze Fernando Pessoa, Portugal's famous poet, sits at a pavement table. Just before you arrive at the café, pop into Livraria Bertrand, fittingly declared the world's oldest operating bookstore by the Guinness Book of World Records.

Rua Serpa Pinto

From Largo do Chiado, press south along Rua Serpa Pinto. You very soon reach a square overlooked by the **Teatro Nacional de São Carlos** ❿ (www.saocarlos.pt), Lisbon's main opera house. This was styled on Milan's La Scala and has a lovely Rococo interior, accessible during performances only. The **Café Lisboa**, see ③, within the theatre, is a performance-inspired delight. Serious foodies who want to experience the culinary genius of José Avillez should cross the road and, if not put off by the sky-high prices, book a table at **Belcanto**, see ④.

A two-minute walk down the street brings you to the **Museu Nacional de Arte Contemporânea do Chiado** or simply the **Museu do Chiado** ⓫ (www.museuartecontemporanea.pt; charge). Stylishly redesigned after the 1988 fire, the museum exhibits mainly Portuguese art from Romanticism through to Modernism. The name is a little misleading, but there are temporary exhibitions with contemporary art on display. There is also a pleasant terrace café where jazz concerts take place in summer.

Café culture

Some say the custom of calling a small black coffee *uma bica* started at *A Brasileira* café. To promote its coffee, which many thought very bitter, the owners placed a placard outside which said *Beba isto com açúcar* (Drink this with sugar). The initials form the word BICA.

Bairro Alto nightlife

Head for the small bars and *tascas* in and around Rua Diario de Noticias late at night and you will probably be able to hear amateur *fado* – *fado vadio* – for the price of a cheap drink. Alternatively, opt for *fado* and dinner. One of the best places is the long-established **O Faia**, see ⑤.

Casa do Ferreira

Rua do Carmo shop

Food and drink

❶ Palácio Chiado

Rua do Alecrim 70;
www.palaciochiado.pt; €€€€

Enjoy gourmet offerings in the historic rooms of the nineteenth-century Quintela Palace, amid frescoes, stained glass and stuccowork. The elegant upstairs restaurant serves sumptuous dishes, spanning lobster to tomahawk steaks, accompanied by an almost out-of-place DJ on Friday and Saturday nights. Continue the dancing in the downstair *SALLA* bar.

❷ A Brasileira

Rua Garrett 120; www.abrasileira.pt; €

Lisbon's most famous (and touristy) café opened in 1905 to sell Brazilian coffee, at that time virtually unknown in Portugal. Every customer who bought a kilo of ground coffee was given a free cup as they waited for their order. It was a favourite haunt of the literati, among them Fernando Pessoa who enjoyed a glass of absinthe and a sweet *bica* while he read or wrote or smoked – his statue sits on the bench out front. It was redesigned in Art Deco style, with a green and gold entrance and a fine interior in wood with mirrors, marble and stuccowork.

❸ Café Lisboa

Teatro Nacional de São Carlos, Largo de São Carlos 23; www.saocarlos.pt; €€

Savour some of Portugal's traditional dishes within Lisbon's opera house – or outside on the square where tables are shaded by white canopies. Beef croquettes, stuffed spider crab or octopus tartar can be followed by roasted codfish, partridge pie, or octopus risotto with coriander, ending with divine *pasteis de nata* (custard tarts). The café and theatre closed for renovations in 2024; re-opening is scheduled for early 2026.

❹ Belcanto

Rua Serpa Pinto 10 A;
www.belcanto.pt; €€€€

This flagship restaurant of famous chef José Avillez, renowned for his culinary creativity, has two Michelin stars and is regarded as the one of the very best restaurants in Portugal. Indeed, it even features in the World's 50 Best Restaurants list. Next door is teeny *Encanto*, Avillez's vegetarian version of his original. Reservations are essential.

❺ O Faia

Rua da Borroca 54–56;
www.ofaia.com; €€€€

This iconic *fado* house, founded in 1947, still boasts big names. You can watch the show over a Portuguese dinner (served until 11pm) but note that the restaurant prices include the show and there is a minimum spend.

Legendary Bairro Alto nightlife

WALK 4
Avenida to the Gulbenkian

A stately boulevard peppered with top designer stores and home to tropical gardens within a park and a museum of world-class art are likely to entice you to this northern sliver of Lisbon.

DISTANCE: 4km (2.5 miles)
TIME: Half a day including visits
START: Praça dos Restauradores (Metro: Restauradores)
END: Gulbenkian Museum
POINTS TO NOTE: This is a good route for a Monday when the Museu Calouste Gulbenkian is open, unlike most of Lisbon's museums. Since the attractions are quite spread out, you might want to use the metro to cut times. There are stops at Avenida, Marquês de Pombal, Parque and São Sebastião, all on the blue line. If you want to visit the Calouste Gulbenkian Museum without the longish walk through the park, take the metro from Marquês de Pombal to São Sebastião. Tables at *Eleven* need to be reserved in advance.

The route takes you along the Avenida da Liberdade, often referred to as Lisbon's Champs-Elysées, through the Parque Eduardo VII and up to the Calouste Gulbenkian Foundation. Of all the foreign visitors to Lisbon during the twentieth century, Calouste Gulbenkian, the Armenian oil magnate, did more for the city than any other. He gave Lisbon the kind of patronage it needed and bequeathed his estate to Portugal on his death in 1955. The foundation, supporting many cultural activities, is a rich and continuing part of Lisbon's fabric. The Calouste Gulbenkian Museum, housing his remarkable art collection, is Lisbon's top museum.

Avenida da Liberdade

From Praça dos Restauradores the **Avenida da Liberdade** ❶ gently slopes uphill for a little over 1km (0.6 mile). This stately boulevard, simply known as the Avenida, was laid out between 1879 and 1882 and is graced with statues, fountains, gardens and pavement cafés, shaded by palm and plane trees. Linking the old town to the new, it is peppered with upmarket hotels, luxury apartments, theatres and – at the upper end – designer stores along the likes of Louis Vuitton, Prada and Emporio Armani. At the top of the Avenida is the huge traffic-

Looking back from the top of Parque Eduardo VII towards the Avenida

girt **Praça Marquês de Pombal** ❷ (or Rotunda) with a bronze Marquês perched on a lofty column, lion by his side, gazing out over the city he rebuilt.

Parque Edouardo VII

Climbing upwards from the roundabout, the **Parque Edouardo VII** ❸ is a park of well-manicured lawns, geometrical box hedges and mosaic-patterned walkways. The formally landscaped gardens were named in honour of Edward VII when he visited Portugal to reaffirm the Anglo-Portuguese alliance in 1903.

On the east side of the park, the **Pavilhão Carlos Lopes** – with tiled panels depicting scenes from Portuguese history – was originally built in Brazil for the Great International Exhibition of Rio de Janeiro in 1922. It was rebuilt in Lisbon in 1932, named the Palácio das Exposições (Palace of Expositions) and adapted for sporting events. In 1984 the name was changed in honour of the Portuguese athlete Carlos Lopes. After a hefty renovation, the building reopened as an events venue in 2017, sometimes hosting candlelit musical concerts.

Praça dos Restauradores

Estufas

In the northwest corner of the park is the **Estufa Fria** ❹ (Cold House; www.informacoeseservicos.lisboa.pt; charge), a horticultural wonderland of exotic plants and flowers, bringing flamboyant relief to the otherwise formal park. The Estufa is entirely covered by green wooden slats which keep out the sun but allow the air to circulate. It is humid without being uncomfortable, and absolutely still – not even the whisper of a breeze. Narrow paths weave their way through flowering shrubs, gigantic palms, colourful flowers and rare trees. Water is everywhere – ponds, small waterfalls, fountains and streams, plus cascades flowing down rock-lined walls. At the far side, a doorway leads through to the cavernous **Estufa Quente** (Hot House), laid out in a similar way and visually just as delightful, but with its glass roof and walls you might find the sticky temperatures and humidity stifling in summer.

The park stretches up to a **belvedere**, with four soaring white columns and fine views over the city, castle and river. Cross the road to the Jardim Amália Rodrigues, named after the *fadista* (1920–99) known as the 'Rainha do *Fado*' or 'Queen of *Fado*' who helped popularise the haunting musical genre worldwide. If you want to treat yourself to something special for lunch (maybe the six-course lobster menu?) try the restaurant **Eleven**, see ❶, or plump for the cheaper option at **Linha d'Água**, see ❷, just to the east (beyond the little bridge), which has a lovely lakeside terrace.

Calouste Gulbenkian

At the dawn of the Oil Age, a far-sighted Turkish-born Armenian put up money to help finance drilling in Mesopotamia, then part of the Turkish Empire. For his part, he received five percent of the Iraq Petroleum Company. Two world wars and the fuelling of millions of cars, planes and ships made Calouste Gulbenkian rich beyond imagination. He became a knowledgeable and dedicated collector of antiquities and great art, beginning with Turkish and Persian carpets, Armenian and Arabic manuscripts and Greek and Roman coins. His passions spread to include ancient Egyptian art, Chinese porcelain and Western painting. His mission was acquiring perfect examples in each of his chosen fields.

Gulbenkian, who held British nationality for much of his life, was preparing to travel to the US when he fell ill in Lisbon. He was so impressed with his treatment here that he decided to stay, establishing a philanthropic foundation to which he left most of his money and his entire art collection when he died in 1955.

Estufa Fria

The belvedere in Parque Eduardo VII

From the gardens, take the cobbled path down to the main road where you will see **El Corte Inglés** ❺, a thirteen-floor shopping centre (part of the Spanish chain) with an excellent supermarket, food hall and gourmet deli. With your back to the department store, walk along the main Avenida de Aguiar until you see a sign for the Fondação Calouste Gulbenkian, just before the major junction. Walk through the park for the museum.

Museu Gulbenkian

Around six thousand items, from antiquity to the early twentieth century, are housed in the **Museu Calouste Gulbenkian** ❻ (Avenida de Berna 45A; www.gulbenkian.pt; charge), created to house one of the finest private art collections in Europe. Calouste Gulbenkian (see box) amassed his works of art over a period of forty years. Born in Istanbul in 1869, he had a passion for fine art and began collecting even before his deals in the oil industry gave him the nickname 'Mr Five Percent'.

Surrounded by its own seventeen-acre park, the museum has spacious galleries with exquisitely presented artefacts. Gulbenkian had very wide-ranging tastes. The **Coleção do Fundador** (Founder's Collection) begins chronologically with Egyptian ceramics and sculptures dating back to around 2700 BC, delicate and perfectly preserved. The handsome statue of the judge Bes is inscribed with hieroglyphs that date it from the reign of Pharaoh Psamtik I (seventh century BC). A large section is devoted to art of the Islamic East and includes ancient fabrics, costumes and carpets, ceramics, glassware and illuminated pages from the Koran.

The survey of Western art begins in the eleventh century with illuminated parchment manuscripts. Tiny ivory sculptures of religious scenes have roots in fourteenth-century France and a number of well-preserved tapestries come from the Flemish and Italian workshops of the sixteenth century. Paintings by Dutch and Flemish masters include works by Rubens, Van der Weyden and Van Dyck, but pride of place goes to two Rembrandts, *Figure of an Old Man* and a painting of a helmeted warrior believed to be Pallas Athene or Alexander the Great, probably modelled on Rembrandt's son Titus.

Don't miss the last room of the museum, devoted to the exquisite Art Nouveau glassware and jewellery designed by René Lalique. Gulbenkian admired it so much that he acquired 169 pieces when he was still young and not particularly rich – by his own standards, of course.

Centro de Arte Moderna

A well-tended park with ponds, paths, sculptures and an outdoor auditorium

Sculpture in the Gulbenkian gardens

Food and drink

1 Eleven
Rua Marquês da Fronteira, Jardim Amália Rodrigues; www.restauranteleven.com; €€€€
Eleven (a nod to the eleven partners who set it up) is helmed by German chef Joachim Koerper. At the top of Eduardo VII Park, it's a minimalist, purpose-built building with picture windows and panoramic views down to the city. Expect exquisite Mediterranean dishes, all made using natural, fresh and seasonal products. Prices are not for the fainthearted.

2 Linha d'Água
Rua Marquês de Fronteira, Jardim Amália Rodrigues; www.linhadeagua.pt; €
Beside a lake at the top of Parque Edouardo VII, this cafeteria provides a peaceful retreat. Come for coffee, snacks and pastries any time of day, or at mealtimes choose from quiches, salads and a couple of fish and meat dishes, ending with a scoop of home-made ice cream.

3 Oh! Lacerda
Avenida de Berna 36A; www.facebook.com/restauranteohlacerda; €€
A quaint, warm and welcoming restaurant serving traditional meat and fish at affordable prices. Steaks are a speciality, and the home-made chips go down a treat. The menu is in Portuguese only, but the friendly staff will help translate.

connects the main Museu Gulbenkian with the combined-ticket **Centro de Arte Moderna Gulbenkian (CAM)** 7, another part of the Gulbenkian Foundation. The museum is dedicated to modern art, dating from the end of the nineteenth century (where the Gulbenkian's collection concludes) to the present day.

The art, which includes installations and sculptures, is mainly Portuguese, though there are also some works by British artists. The collection continues to grow and is displayed on a rotating basis. The most famous painting is the portrait of the poet *Fernando Pessoa in the Café Irmãos Unidos* (1964) by José de Almada Negreiros. Much of the space is dedicated to temporary exhibitions of contemporary art. The museum has a popular café with an outdoor terrace area overlooking the gardens.

If you've had your fill of culture for the day, wind down with a little retail therapy in the Corte Inglés shopping centre or perhaps refuel with some hearty Portuguese cuisine at **Oh! Lacerda** see 3, very close to the museum.

A Turner at the Gulbenkian

The Gulbenkian is home to extensive artworks

WALK 5
South from Estrela

Wander through the well-heeled neighbourhoods of Estrela and Lapa, browse a world-class museum of ancient art, then dive into the cobbled backstreets of Madragoa. The lively riverside docas are an option for night owls.

DISTANCE: 3.5km (2 miles)
TIME: Half a day, with visits
START: Basilica da Estrela
END: Madragoa (or docas)
POINTS TO NOTE: For Estrela take Bus 774 from Praça do Comércio, or Tram 25 or 28. The museums included are closed on a Monday.

To the west of central Lisbon, this quarter sees fewer tourists than Alfama, Baixa or Bairro Alto. The route starts in the leafy Estrela district, then shifts south to Lapa, an elegant residential neighbourhood with embassies and desirable residences overlooking the Tagus. The Museu Nacional de Arte Antiga provides a comprehensive view of Portuguese art from the twelfth to the nineteenth centuries. The route also takes in the Madragoa neighbourhood, formerly a quarter of fishermen.

Basílica da Estrela

Poised on a hill, the enormous domed **Basílica da Estrela** ❶ (Praça da Estrela; www.visitlisboa.com; church free, terrace charge) is one of Lisbon's great landmarks. The church was built between 1779 and 1790 at the behest of Queen Maria I to fulfil a vow she had made for the birth of a son. Sadly, he died of smallpox two years before the completion of the church. Maria never got over his passing and died in Brazil in 1816. She lies in grandeur in the right transept, in a particularly morbid affair of black marble, decorated with a writhing serpent, mourning angels and marble skulls. Tucked away in a small room is an enormous **nativity scene** carved by Machado de Castro, composed of over five hundred cork and terracotta figures. A climb up 114 steps to the **terrace** is rewarded with sweeping views over Lisbon.

Opposite the Basilica, the delightful **Jardim da Estrela** ❷ (Estrela Gardens; free) is very much a neighbourhood park, where children enjoy the duck ponds and playground and older residents pass the time of day chatting on shady

View from the top of Basílica da Estrela

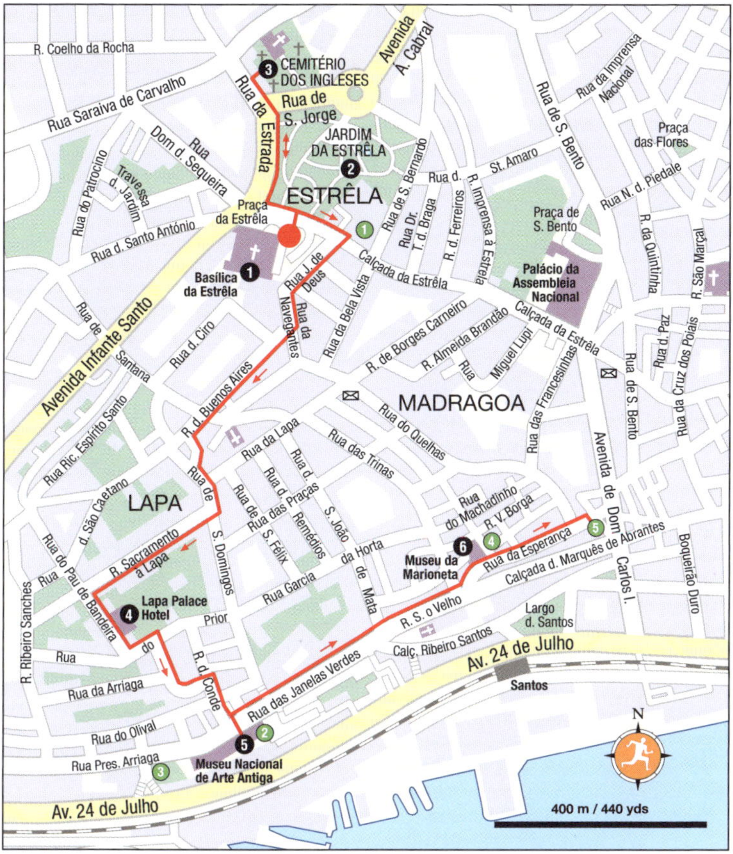

benches. The tranquil gardens have lofty plane trees, subtropical plants, swathes of agapanthus and almost sufficient birdsong to drown out traffic noise from surrounding streets.

Cemitério dos Ingleses

Just north of the gardens lies the **Cemitério dos Ingleses** ❸ (English Cemetery; Rua São Jorge; donations welcomed). To reach the cemetery, leave

Basílica da Estrela

the gardens at Rua da Estrela, turn right and then right again for the Rua São Jorge. The burial site of the Anglican St George's Church, this is a leafy oasis with tree-shaded graves, set among box hedges. A sign leads you to the raised tomb of the eighteenth-century novelist and playwright Henry Fielding, who came to Lisbon to improve his health, but died only two months later in 1754 at the age of 47. No one knows the exact spot where he was laid to rest, but a monument was erected to him in 1830. It is believed British soldiers were buried here during the Peninsular War, but there are no marked graves. The Commonwealth War Graves commemorate servicemen who died in the Lisbon area during World War II.

Return to Praça da Estrela, and for a caffeine break try the simple *Doce Estrela* across the little park from the basilica. Practice your Portuguese (little English is spoken here) and enjoy good coffee and cakes. Take the Rua João de Deus (beside the café), then head down Rua dos Navigantes and into Rua de Buenos Aires. Turn left into Rua São Domingos, then right along the tranquil **Rua do Sacramento à Lapa**, which is full of elegant embassies. A left at Rua do Pau al Bandiera will bring you to the **Lapa Palace Hotel** ❹, a lovely spot for a coffee or cocktail if you're feeling flush. At the junction turn left, then first right (Rua da São Francisco de Borja) and continue downhill for the square with the marble fountain.

Museu Nacional de Arte Antiga

Across the square is the **Museu Nacional de Arte Antiga** ❺ (National Museum of Ancient Art; www.museudearteantiga.pt; charge), Portugal's major art museum, with several masterpieces of international renown. It is spread across three floors of a handsomely designed palace, though don't be surprised to find at least some of the rooms closed for lack of staff.

Level 1 is dedicated to textiles, furniture and paintings by foreign artists, including Tiepolo, Dürer (a self-portrait and hypnotic *Saint Jerome*) and, most strikingly, the Spaniard Francisco de Zurbarán, whose six larger-than-life saints once belonged to the monastery of São Vicente de Fora (see page 31). The same floor also has a macabre and fascinating triptych by Hieronymus Bosch. *The Temptation of St Anthony* (c.1500) is a fantastic hallucination, tempered with humour and executed with genius. A crane rigged up like a helicopter, flying fish taxis and horse-size rats fill this ghoulish nightmare.

Level 2 displays some exquisite pieces from East Asia, including ceramics, gold, silverware and jewellery, much of it from the Portuguese discoveries of the fifteenth and sixteenth centuries. Two finely executed Japanese *Namban* screens depict the moment that the Portuguese set foot in southern Japan in 1543 – the first Europeans to do so.

Cemitério dos Ingleses

The top floor is devoted to Portuguese art and sculpture. The highlight here is the **Polyptych of St Vincent**, attributed to the fifteenth-century Portuguese master, Nuno Gonçalves, official painter to King Afonso V. It is a spectacular portrait of contemporary dignitaries, with masterful attention to detail of the individuals. Fifty-eight figures are gathered around St Vincent, among them Prince Henry the Navigator (to the left of St Vincent in the third panel from the left) in his large black hat and possibly Nuno Gonçalves himself up in the top left corner. Other figures are shown in every range of mood – ire, boredom, amusement – while several of the assembled clergymen appear as ugly, evil or both.

Revive yourself with liquid refreshment or lunch on the lovely terrace of the **museum café**, see 1, or at the modern **Catch Me**, see 2, just below the museum on the riverside.

Turn right out of the museum, along the Rua Janelas Verdes, then take the left fork by the large pink Igreja de Santos-o-Velho. Another left fork brings you into Rua da Esperanza.

Museu da Marioneta

Just up the hill is the **Museu da Marioneta** 6 (Puppet Museum; www.museudamarioneta.pt; charge), with its collection of puppets in all shapes and sizes, beautifully displayed in rooms off the cloisters of the former Convento das Bernardas. Crafted from gold leaf, papier mâché, wood, metal, leather, snail shell, camel or buffalo hide, the designs come from all over the world: Khon masks from Thailand; rod puppets from Java and Sicily; shadow puppets from China, Japan and Turkey; marionettes from Myanmar; and glove puppets from Italy and England. The oldest come from Asia and date back to the sixteenth century. Videos and touchscreens show puppets in action (including Punch and Judy) and demonstrations of the painstaking creation of the models. The cloisters are the setting for the romantic restaurant **Fado No Convento**, see 3, open for dinner only. Book a table for later if it appeals.

Duck down the streets behind the Rua da Esperança for a full flavour of the atmospheric Madragoa quarter, with its fading facades, overflowing flowerpots and tiny groceries and bars. From the museum take the first left along the Calçada do Castelo Picão and then right to explore the **Rua das Madres** and surrounding streets. At the end of the road head right (Traversa do Pasteleiro) to rejoin the Rua de Esperança.

For a slap-up fish lunch or dinner continue along Rua de Esperança, which joins the main Avenida Dom Carlos 1, then swerve right for **Frade dos Mares**, see 4 at No 55.

Alcântara

For nightlife on the river, trendy *aperitivos* or more museums, head

Museu Nacional de Arte Antiga

Bosch's *Temptation of St Anthony*

Food and drink

1 Museu Nacional de Arte Antiga Restaurant
Rua das Janelas Verdes 122; www.museudearteantiga.pt; €€
The highlight here is the irresistible garden terrace over the Tagus, dotted with statues and fountains. There is not a huge choice of main courses but what's on offer (pasta and at least one fish or meat dish) is wholesome and excellent value.

2 Catch Me
Jardim 9 de Abril 18–20; www.catch-me.pt; €€€
Just below the Museu Nacional de Arte Antiga, with a spacious terrace overlooking the river, this is an inviting, modern spot for a cocktail, perhaps to the soundtrack of a sunset DJ. The menu is international.

3 Fado No Convento
Travessa do Convento das Bernardas 12; www.fadonoconvento.com; €€€€
The candlelit restaurant has an alluring setting within a former eighteenth-century convent, and tables are laid out in the cloisters on warm summer evenings. The *fado* performances are as Portuguese as you get, but the menu is fancifully French, with sautéed scallops, duck confit and first-class steaks.

4 Frade dos Mares
Avenida Dom Carlos 1, 55A; www.facebook.com/FradedosMares; €€
This small, friendly restaurant has stylish modern decor and delicious, ever-changing fish dishes, which might include mussels au gratin, octopus cataplana with sweet potato or tuna tataki. Carnivores can tuck into steak, duck or pork; vegetarians into plant-based risottos.

west to Alcântara. The arrival of the **LX Factory** cultural hub in 2008, followed by the requalification of the quarter's buildings, particularly the opening of the palace-housed **Museu de Arte Contemporânea Armando Martins** (MACAM; www.macam.pt) in 2025, have put this district firmly on the radar. Buses and trams trundle along Avenida 24 de Julho, aptly towards the **Museu da Carris** (Tram Museum; www.museu.carris.pt).

For a riverside refreshment, head to the docas: **Doca de Santo Amaro**, beneath the huge Ponte 25 de April suspension bridge, or the neighbouring, less intimate, **Doca de Alcântara**. These stylishly converted dockside warehouses have been reimagined as creative hubs and venues for bars, cafés, clubs and restaurants. Relax by the river by day, dine or party at night (some clubs don't close until 6am at weekends).

The LX factory is a cultural hub with a rooftop bar

TOUR 6
Belém

No visit to Lisbon is complete without at least one day in Belém, where exuberant masterpieces of the Manueline stand as symbols of the Age of Discoveries. There is a wealth of museums, too, as well as a riverside setting, inviting parks and tranquil gardens.

DISTANCE: 7km (4.3 miles) by tram to Belém; walking tour: 3km (2 miles)
TIME: A very full day, ideally two.
START: Praça da Figueira
END: Belém
POINTS TO NOTE: For transport to Belém, alternatives to the recommended Tram 15 are bus #714, or suburban train line from Cais do Sodré. Don't visit on Monday when most monuments and museums are closed. The Royal Palace is only open on Saturdays. The main tourist attractions, especially the monastery, can get impossibly busy in peak season and at weekends so try to arrive either earlier or later in the day. You are unlikely to fit in all the sights suggested in the route in a day. Set off early and, if time is pressing, skip the monastery museums. Several combined tickets are available, covering various Belém attractions. If you are planning to eat at *Feitora* (see Food and drink) reserve a table.

Belém, 6km (4 miles) west of the city centre at the mouth of the River Tagus, is a spacious suburb whose abundance of monuments, museums, palaces and gardens makes it one of the most popular areas for visitors. Although the shore has changed beyond recognition, it was from the river at Belém that the Portuguese explorers set out in the fifteenth and sixteenth centuries. In 1487 Bartolomeu Dias embarked on the voyage that would take him round the Cape of Good Hope, opening the sea route to India, and it was also from the Tejo shore that Vasco Da Gama embarked on his journey in 1497, after praying in a small chapel built by Henry the Navigator. The chapel was levelled shortly afterwards and, in its place, arose the great Mosteiro dos Jerónimos. Along with Belém's famous monuments is an ever-growing crop of diverse museums along the revamped riverfront, which is delightful to stroll. The state-of-the-art MAAT (Museum of Art, Architecture and Technology) and Quake, a virtual experience recreating the 1755 earthquake, are worth a visit.

Torre de Belém

Buses may be quicker to Belém, but more fun is the sleek modern Tram 15 (marked #15E, Algés), which departs from Praça da Figueira four to six times an hour. It also stops at Praça do Comércio and Cais do Sodré but you are more likely to secure a seat by taking it from the departure point. You can buy a ticket on the bus or use a pre-paid Viva Viagem card, which is cheaper. The journey follows the course of the Tagus and takes 25 to forty minutes depending on traffic. Alight at the first Belém stop for the National Coach Museum and MAAT.

Museu Nacional dos Coches

A unique collection of over seventy fine carriages, many drawn by royal horses on ceremonial occasions over four centuries, can be seen at the The **Museu Nacional dos Coches** ❶ (National Coach Museum; Praça Afonso de Albuquerque; www.museudoscoches.gov.pt; charge). The display is housed across two buildings. The grandest, the former riding arena of Belém Palace, designed as a school for Lusitano horses, became the world's first coach museum under Queen Amélia (1865–1951), wife of King Carlos I. In 2015, a second, purpose-built building was inaugurated across the street, which now houses the bulk of the collection.

Especially imposing are the huge carriages commissioned by King João V – one for his own use, and three for the Grand Legation to Pope Clement XI – with their extravagant groups of carved and gilded Baroque-style figures. The coach used by King José I, the berlin made for Queen Maria

The Old Riding Hall of the Museu Nacional dos Coches

for the inauguration of the Basílica da Estrela, a charming eighteenth-century French litter and the miniature carriage used by King Carlos I as a child are among the elegant exhibits.

Palácio Real de Belém

After the coach museum you could cross over the railway line and busy N6 (use the pedestrian bridge) to see contemporary exhibitions at **MAAT** (see box) or venture over the main Rua Belém to the guard-flanked **Palácio Real de Belém** ❷ (Praça Afonso de Albuquerque; www.museu.presidencia.pt; charge). A palace has stood here for five centuries, and from when it was purchased by João V in 1726 until the late nineteenth century it housed successive generations of kings and queens. The building survived the earthquake of 1755, witnessed the departure of the royal family to Brazil in 1807 and saw the deaths of several princes. It is now the official residence of the President of Portugal. The Changing of the Guard, in which horses parade and bands play, is held in front of the palace at 11am on the third Sunday of the month. The abode is open to the public on Saturdays for guided tours only, which take in the gardens as well as rooms inside. Within the building is the **Museo da Presidência da República** (Museum of the President of the Republic), with more regular opening hours, but unless you are heavily into modern Portuguese history, press on to try the most famous *pasteis de nata* (custard tarts) in Lisbon at **Pastéis de Belém**, see ❶. Sample a couple with coffee before continuing along the main street for the monastery.

Mosteiro dos Jerónimos

Thanks to wealth garnered from the spice trade and profit made from maritime exploration and colonisation, King Manuel was the richest king in Christendom. The most striking legacy of his remarkable reign, in which tiny Portugal dominated far oceans, is the **Mosteiro dos Jerónimos** ❸ (Jerónimos Monastery; Praça do Império; www.museusemonumentos.pt; cloisters charge, church free). King Manuel laid the cornerstone of the Hieronymite monastery in 1502, on the site of the chapel founded by Prince Henry the Navigator.

Interior

The monastery, declared a National Monument in 1907 and a World Heritage Site in 1983, is Lisbon's largest and most dazzling religious monument. The Manueline style (see box, page 63) gives it its striking individuality. The convent wing was destroyed in the 1755 earthquake, but the church and cloister survive. The south portal is a brilliant example of the Manueline stonework, with intricately carved gables, pinnacles, saints – and possibly Henry the Navigator (though some historians disagree) on the central

Cloisters at Mosteiro dos Jerónimos

pedestal. Crowning the portal on a pedestal at the top is the Madonna, Santa Maria de Belém (Bethlehem).

The interior is lofty and harmonious with slender, ornately decorated columns covered with vines and shoots, rising like palm trees to a graceful vaulted roof. The effect is one of immense height and space. Just inside the entrance, on the left, is the nautical-themed tomb of Vasco da Gama who died in Cochin and, opposite, another tomb honours poet Luís de Camões, whose epic poem *Os Lusíadas (The Lusiads)* recounts the story of Portugal's early navigators and their maritime explorations. The great poet was actually buried in a pauper's grave in 1580.

In the chancel are the tombs of King Manuel I, King João III and their queens (Manuel married three times; it is his second wife, mother of his ten children, who lies here). Elephants, symbol of power and a tribute to the newly discovered marvels of East Asia, support the sarcophagi. In the south transept lies the empty tomb of King Sebastião I whose death in 1578 brought the Avis dynasty to an end. The young king never returned from battle in North Africa.

Cloister

Turn right out of the church, purchase a ticket for the cloister and join the queue. It is well worth the wait. This is an exquisite and airy two-level structure of strikingly original proportions and perspectives. Exuberant sculptural detail decorates every arch, column and even the walls. The adjoining refectory, lined with Rococo *azulejos*, makes a fine setting for occasional concerts. Upstairs, there are good views down into the church and cloisters – as well as a bookshop and information on the history of the monastery.

If you only have a day to visit to Belém you may have to skip the monastery museums (Archaeology and Maritime) or, if you would rather concentrate on the old rather than the new, skip the Museu de Arte Contemporânea (see below). A lovely spot for lunch is the **Rua Vieira Portuense**, with its row of colourful sixteenth- and seventeenth-century houses, and terraces overlooking the river. Take your pick of the restaurants, most of which serve authentic Portuguese fare. **O Caniço**, see 2, is a good bet.

Museu Nacional de Arqueologia

The monastery stretches to the west, in more modern additions. The **Museu Nacional de Arqueologia** 4 (www.museunacionalarqueologia.gov.pt; charge) hosts temporary exhibitions along with a permanent collection, shown on a rotating basis, of finds from all over Portugal dating back to the Iron Age. The exquisite **Egyptian Antiquities** span five thousand years, from prehistory to the Coptic period (AD 395–642), and the now-reopened

Mosteiro dos Jerónimos' striking white building

Tesouros da Arqueologia Portuguesa (Treasures of Portuguese Archaeology) is a permanent exhibition with stunning bronze and gold jewellery from the third-millennium BC, including many examples of torcs.

Museu da Marinha

Portugal's fascinating maritime heritage is documented at the **Museu da Marinha** ❺, housed in the monastery and newer buildings around the Praça do Império. The journey follows the story of the Portuguese explorers and their epic journeys east. A large statue of Henry the Navigator stands in the main entrance in what was once a chapel built by him, where mariners took mass before their departure to the high seas. The oldest item in the museum is the delightful wooden figure of the Archangel St Raphael, which accompanied Vasco da Gama to India and was brought back to Lisbon in 1600 by one of his great grandsons.

Exhibits include models of ships down the ages, navigational equipment, maritime paintings, erstwhile votos and replicas of sixteenth-century maps. From more recent times are the handsome royal suites from the *Amália*, the 1901 royal yacht named after Portugal's last queen. Pride of place goes to the huge galliot, or brigantine, built in 1785 to celebrate a royal marriage with seats for eighty oarsmen. The last time it was on the river Tagus was in 1957, carrying Queen Elizabeth II on a state visit. Next to it is the seaplane piloted by Portuguese aviators that made the first flight across the South Atlantic in 1922.

Manueline architecture

The Portuguese may be principally known for *azulejo* designs and port wine, but equally important is the ornate style of architecture and stone carving that suddenly appeared in Portugal in the late fifteenth century. It flourished for only a few decades, mostly during the reign of Manuel I (1495–1521), hence the name Manueline. Probably triggered by the great ocean voyages of discovery, it took late Gothic as its base but added fanciful decoration and dramatic touches that were frequently references to the sea. Stone was carved like knotted rope and sculpted into imitation coral, seahorse, nets and waves, as well as non-nautical designs. The style first appeared in the small Igreja de Jesus in Setúbal (see page 93), then in the Torre de Belém and the monastery. It reached a peak of complexity in the unfinished chapels of the monastery at Batalha, between Lisbon and Coimbra. In the early sixteenth century, the style fell out of favour, and by 1540 Portugal had joined the rest of Europe in building in the more sober Renaissance style.

MAAT

Opened in 2016, Lisbon's sleek cultural hub looms above the riverside in Belém alongside the twentieth-century Tejo Power Station. The MAAT (Museum for Art, Architecture and Technology; Edificio Central Tejo, Avenida de Brasília; www.maat.pt; charge) is a striking contemporary building, resembling a gently rising wave, which you can walk over, under and through. It was designed by Stirling Prize-winning British architect Amanda Levete as an exhibition centre for the works of internationally renowned modern and contemporary artists and architects. The exhibits include the EDP Foundation Art Collection, with works by Portuguese artists dating back to the 1960s. MAAT also incorporates the iconic red-brick Tejo Power Station, which has eight galleries hosting temporary exhibitions. This was the largest power plant in Portugal until the 1950s. Though the building has been restored, the steam engines, hydraulic generators and vast British-manufactured *caldeiras* (boilers) remain on view to the public.

Museu de Arte Contemporânea (MAC/CCB)

South of the monastery in the main square lies the **Centro Cultural de Belém** ❻ (CCB). Built in 1992, the centre has a strong cultural programme and is home to the **Museu de Arte Contemporânea** (www.ccb.pt; charge), formerly known as the Berardo Collection, boasting one of the world's largest curations of modern and contemporary art.

The displays present a journey of art through the twentieth century to the present day via its most significant movements and protagonists. Around nine hundred works of art are spread across three floors, against gleaming white walls in a minimalist setting. The exhibits are set out with striking chronological clarity, starting with Picasso and the invention of Cubism and ending with American Pop Art, featuring Andy Warhol's *Brillo Boxes*. The illustrious roll call of modern greats includes Picasso, Dalí, Piet Mondrian, Joan Miró and Francis Bacon. There is a choice of bars and restaurants, including **ÚNICO**, see ③.

Padrão dos Descobrimentos

From the Centro Cultural take the underpass to the **Padrão dos Descobrimentos** ❼ (Monument to the Discoveries; www.padraodos descobrimentos.pt; charge). Jutting from the riverbank like a caravel cresting a wave, it was built in 1960 to commemorate the 500th anniversary of Prince Henry the Navigator's death. Erected during the Salazar regime, the design has rarely been admired but there's a certain intrigue about

The wave-like architecture of MAAT

the sea-facing stone figures. On the prow stands Henry, looking out to the waves beyond; the figures behind represent the explorers, mariners, crusaders, astronomers, cartographers and chroniclers that were instrumental in Portugal's Age of Exploration. The leaflet that comes with the ticket shows you exactly who's who on the monument. Inside, you can take a lift followed by stairs for fine views of the city and river. From here you can also spot the Rosa dos Ventos (Compass Rose), a vast black-and-red limestone map of the world at the foot of the monument, with key dates of journeys.

Torre de Belém

Walk along the waterfront westwards as far as the **Torre de Belém** 8 (Belém Tower; www.visitlisboa.com; charge), a UNESCO World Heritage Site. This exquisite little fortress, erected to guard the entrance of the Tagus, is picturesquely set on the edge of the river, the site where Vasco da Gama and other navigators set forth on their explorations. Built between 1514 and 1520, it is a fine example of the Manueline style, with its richly carved niches, corner turrets and shields bearing the Templar cross. Inside, you can peer into a dungeon and climb the tower for fine river views, but its true charm is appreciated from the outside. It must have been a wonderful sight to weary explorers returning from their perilous journeys.

Come dusk enjoy a cocktail at a waterside bar, watch Belém glow in the setting sun and the light fade over the river. For dinner you could splash out on one of the smart restaurants at the **Doca do Bom Sucesso** 9, the small marina east of the tower and a popular night spot. **Feitora**, see 4, at the *Altis Belém Hotel* has a Michelin star. Alternatively, riverside kiosks dish up light bites or you could head back to one of the restaurants along Rua Veira Portuense for a simple seafood supper.

Palácio Nacional da Ajuda

If you have a couple of hours to spare, consider a visit to the **Palácio Nacional da Ajuda** (Largo da Ajuda; www.palacioajuda.gov.pt; charge), just over 1km (0.6 mile) north of the Museu dos Coches. It's quite a hike on a hot day up the Calçada da Ajuda but a taxi from the square below will whisk you there in a couple of minutes. The palace is colossal. Work began in 1802 to replace the temporary wooden palace erected here after the earthquake, but the royal family left soon afterwards for Brazil, and the palace, which was planned to be double the size of the present one, was never completed. However, under King Luis I's Italian bride, Maria Pia of Savoy, it saw lavish trappings including Gobelin tapestries, East Asian ceramics, crystal chandeliers, rare Portuguese furniture, artworks and curiosities. Important state ceremonies are still held here. Over the road is the

Padrão dos Descobrimentos

The landmark Torre de Belém

Food and drink

1 Pastéis de Belém

Rua de Belém 84–92; www.pasteisdebelem.pt; €

This long-standing institution is famous for its *pastéis de nata* (custard tarts). The relatively small shopfront belies a warren of rooms, all lined with blue-and-white *azulejos*. Here, locals and visitors alike drink good coffee and enjoy the oven-warm delicate pieces of heaven, made to a secret recipe. You can also buy to take away but be prepared to queue.

2 O Caniço

Rua Vieira Portuense 30–32; www.facebook.com/RestauranteBelemCanico; €

Join the locals on the terrace overlooking gardens in this simple family-run restaurant. The fish and seafood here are excellent value. Try the *pasteis de bacalhau* (salt-cod fritters), the *açorda de gambas* (bread soup with prawns and coriander), fresh scabbard fish or skewers of octopus and prawns, served with salad and delicious potatoes in garlic and olive oil.

3 ÚNICO

Centro Cultural de Belém, Praça do Império; www.gruposushicafe.pt; €€

Within the Centro Cultural de Belém, this café specialises in organic dishes ranging from soups and pizzas to poké bowls and pasta. The setting is light and airy, with plenty of plants to bring nature inside. The café was established as a social-impact organisation, focusing on providing training and employment opportunities to persons with learning disabilities.

4 Feitora

Altis Belém Hotel & Spa, Doca do Bom Successo; www.restaurantefeitoria.com; €€€€

Save this one for a special evening occasion. Chef André Cruz's cuisine is inspired by the spirit of the Portuguese explorers and his beautifully presented dishes combine traditional Portuguese flavours with Asian influences. The restaurant is spacious and contemporary, with superb river views.

Jardim Botânico da Ajuda, formal Italianate gardens, with five thousand plant species from all over the world.

Equestrian shows

From April to November the **Escola Portuguesa de Art Equestre** (Portuguese school of Equestrian Art), based at Queluz, trains Lusitano horses and holds training sessions and performances at the Henrique Calado Riding Ring in Calçada da Ajuda, Belém. For tickets and schedules visit www.parquesdesintra.pt.

The Marble Room of Palácio Nacional da Ajuda

WALK 7
Parque das Nações (Park of Nations)

This former wasteland was transformed for Expo 98 and couldn't be more different from the hilly city centre: a flat landscape studded with high-rise pavilions, a spacious waterfront and one of the best aquariums in the world.

DISTANCE: 2.2km (1.4 miles; or more if you take in the Parque do Tejo)
TIME: Half a day
START: Oriente station
END: Parque do Tejo
POINTS TO NOTE: Arrive early for the Oceanarium and book tickets online (www.oceanario.pt); the queues are particularly long on summer weekends. Set aside plenty of time for this attraction – many people spend half a day here. Take the metro red line from central Lisbon to Oriente station (around twenty minutes) or (much slower) bus #728 from Praça do Comércio. The Oceanarium has a café and restaurant; the park has a choice of affordable eateries; while the Vasco da Gama mall has cafés and bars, and a supermarket.

You might just see the park as a soulless concrete strip, fading at the edges. Or you might view it as a great day out with the kids: a stunning science museum, pedestrianised walkways, cycle paths and cable cars that glide above the park and river. It's also popular with aficionados of contemporary architecture thanks to its stunning Oriente station and striking waterfront pavilions. Further south, neighbouring Marvila and Beato are emerging as bohemian-cool districts.

Expo legacy

Prior to Expo 98, the eastern end of the Lisbon waterfront was an ugly, derelict industrial site. Held on the 500th anniversary of Vasco da Gama's voyage to India, the Expo sparked a flurry of revitalisation, with some of the world's most innovative architects creating a high-tech entertainment and leisure zone, along with new shopping and nightlife. The theme was The Oceans, a Heritage for the Future. Framing the park is the futuristic railway station, a pristine shopping centre and the sleek white Ponte Vasco da Gama (Vasco da Gama Bridge), leaping across the Tagus.

The metro surfaces at the mainline station, **Estação do Oriente ❶**, with its stunning top-level glass roof, the brainchild of Spanish architect

Estação do Oriente's bold exterior

Santiago Calatrava. Walk through the **Centro Vasco da Gama** ❷ shopping centre (Avenida Dom João II 40; www.centrovascodagama.pt), another design by Calatrava, with viewing terraces back and front, overlooking the station and towards the river.

The Parque das Nações extends 5km (3 miles) along the riverfront. Runners pound the waterfront, passing fisherfolk casting their lines into the Tagus, though most tourists head straight for the oceanarium.

Oceanário

Head south along the Alameda dos Oceanos for the **Oceanário de Lisboa** ❸ (Oceanarium; www.oceanario.pt; charge). Designed by American architect Peter Chermayeff and surrounded by water, the structure resembles a marooned oil derrick or space station from the set of a sci-fi thriller. Reached by a footbridge, it houses large tanks representing four distinct marine ecosystems: Antarctic, Indian, Pacific and Atlantic, but creating the illusion of a single aquarium and a sole ocean.

There are over eight thousand sea creatures in seven million litres of saltwater. You'll see Magellanic and crested rockhopper penguins in the Antarctic section and sea otters in the Pacific (there are otters named Eusébio after the football player and Amália after the *fado* singer Amália Rodrigues). As visitors make their way around the massive circular aquarium, tiger sharks, manta rays and schools of exotic fish glide by, overhead and beneath the observation decks. It is one of the few aquariums in the world to house the huge ocean sunfish.

Oceanário de Lisboa

Visit the website for activities from guided tours to a sleepover with sharks.

Pavilhão do Conhecimento

On the Alameda dos Oceanos, just inland and south from the Oceanarium, the **Pavilhão do Conhecimento** ❹ (Pavilion of Knowledge; www.pavconhecimento.pt; charge) is an interactive science and technology museum with fascinating exhibitions and thrilling experiments for all ages. Beyond the museum, the **Jardins da Água** (Water Gardens) has water jets, waterfalls and benches under palm trees and provides a cool retreat in mid-summer.

The waterfront

For a bird's-eye view over the river and park, take the **Telecabine** ❺ (cable car; www.telecabinelisboa.pt; charge) from the Oceanarium to the Vasco da Gama Tower – with the option of a return trip. Alternatively, it's a pleasant walk along the riverside promenade, on the east side of the Doca dos Oliviais. This runs all the way to the Vasco da Gama Bridge.

Overlooking the **Olivais Dock** is the prize-winning **Pavilhão de Portugal** ❻, a multipurpose arena designed by leading Portuguese architect Álvaro Siza Vieira. The pavilion has an astonishing curved concrete roof, suspended over its forecourt. Beyond it you'll see one of the many notable artworks in the park: Antony Gormley's iron statue *Rhizome*, representing nine figures. North of the marina, the space ship-like **MEO Arena** ❼ (formerly the Pavilhão Atlântico) can host up to 20,000 spectators and is Portugal's largest indoor arena and venue for sporting events.

You'll find a variety of lunch options along the **Rua da Pimenta**, bordered by terraces with views of the **Jardim Garcia da Orta** ❽ and the river. **Senhor Peixe**, see ①, and **Restaurante D'Bacalhau**, see ②, are the best bets for fish. Another option is a picnic in the **Parque do Tejo**, a large park with bike trails and riverside walks unfurling beyond the 150m (492ft) -high **Torre Vasco da Gama** ❾

Trendy new neighbours

Since the early 2020s, the formerly industrial Marvila and Beato quarters, just south of Parque das Nações, have quickly become Lisbon's hippest areas and are a great place to end the day. Old warehouses have been converted into temporary and permanent cultural centres and galleries, such as 8 Marvila in the Marvila Art District (www.madmarvila.pt) and the Fábrica Braço de Prata (www.fabricabracodeprata.com), a quirky restaurant, bar and cultural hub. Craft breweries and taprooms are continuously popping up – cavernous *Dois Corvos* (www.doiscorvos.pt) is one of the best.

Food and drink

1 Senhor Peixe
Rua da Pimenta 35;
www.senhorpeixe.pt; €€€
The lobsters in the tank and wonderful array of fish inside are likely to lure you into *Senhor Peixe* (Mr Fish). Usually buzzing with Portuguese, the restaurant offers around twenty different types of fish, mostly priced by the kilo. Among the specialities are *arroz de lagosta* (lobster risotto), *choco frito* (fried cuttlefish) and a wonderful *caldeirada* (fish stew) for two. Reserve a table on the terrace for river views across the gardens.

2 Restaurante D'Bacalhau
Rua Pimenta 45;
www.restaurantebacalhau.com; €€
Bacalhau (salted cod) is king at this restaurant, steps away from the Tagus. It is served in around ten different ways, from *lagueirada de bacalhau* with egg, spinach and chickpeas to the popular *com natas*, baked in cream sauce with potatoes. You can try a selection of four by opting for *mezcla de bacalhau* (codfish mix, for a minimum of two). Other options are skewers of grouper, braised salmon or grilled octopus.

3 River Lounge
Cais das Naus, Lote 2.21.01;
www.myriad.pt; €€€
If you want to be right on the river, head for the glass-walled *River Lounge* restaurant of the *Myriad by Sana Hotel*, located on the Tagus with fine views of the Vasco da Gama Bridge and Mediterranean-inspired cuisine. The setting is contemporary, the service professional.

(Vasco da Gama Tower). Formerly part of an oil refinery, the tower was fashioned to look like a caravel. It is now integrated into the luxury **Myriad by Sana Hotel**, whose restaurant, see 3, has fine views of the estuary.

Ponte Vasco da Gama

The massive 17.2km (10.75 miles) **Ponte Vasco da Gama**, spanning the Tagus is the longest bridge in Europe. A second bridge had become essential to alleviate the congestion on the Ponte 25 de Abril. To finance it, the Portuguese government commissioned a private consortium, Lusoponte, who hold exclusive control of toll collection of both Lisbon's bridges for forty years.

The bridge, completed in three years just in time for Expo 98, is designed to withstand tremors 4.5 times stronger than the 1755 earthquake. Before the opening it set a Guinness world record for amassing 15,000 Portuguese to feast on the largest *feijoada* (bean stew) ever, served at a 3 mile (5km) -long table.

Ponte Vasco da Gama at sunrise

TOUR 8
Cristo Rei

Set on the south bank of the Tagus, the Cristo Rei monument is so big you're bound to spy it at some stage during your visit to Lisbon; but it's fun to take the ferry across for a sensational panorama from the 82 metre (269ft)-high viewing platform.

DISTANCE: Ferry (return trip) 6km (4 miles), Bus (return trip) 7km (4.4 miles)
TIME: A half-day
START: Cais do Sodré
END: Cacilhas
POINTS TO NOTE: Choose a clear bright day. Ferries depart from Cais do Sodré at least four times an hour. Try to avoid weekends and returning during rush hour (5–7.30pm). There are often long queues for the lift up the Cristo Rei but, even at ground level, the views are spectacular. If you visit the Cristo Rei in the morning, you could always take a bus from Cacilhas to the Costa da Caparica (approximately 35 minutes), home to some of the most pleasant beaches in the Lisbon area.

Cristo Rei: a Lisbon landmark

Lisboetas call it Outra Banda, the other shore, meaning the other bank of the River Tejo, long neglected because of the inconvenience of reaching it. This changed after 1966 with the completion of what was then Europe's longest suspension bridge, the Ponte 25 de Abril, and made even easier with the opening of the rail link in 1999. A second bridge, the Vasco da Gama, opened in 1998 to relieve the ever-growing pressure on the original.

Echoing the iconic Christ the Redeemer statue in Rio de Janeiro, the Cristo Rei stands high above Lisbon

The mighty Cristo Rei

across the river, just west of the Ponte 25 de Abril. The monument was built between 1949 and 1959 under the Salazar dictatorship as a sign of gratitude to God for saving Portugal from involvement in World War II.

How to get there

At **Cais do Sodré** ❶ follow signs for the Terminal Fluvial (Ferry Terminal). Buy a return ticket, or use your tap-on Lisbon pass, to **Cacilhas** ❷, hopping on one of the orange ferries and enjoy the fifteen-minute ride. Cacilhas itself is nothing to write home about but it is a popular weekend and evening destination for Lisboetas thanks to its abundance of seafood restaurants. *Caldeirada a fragateira*, a tasty fish stew, is a speciality, as are piles of fresh sardines, often cooked on smoking grills outdoors.

From Cacilhas you can take a taxi or the #101 bus, which departs regularly for the Cristo Rei monument, where it terminates.

Ponte 25 de Abril with Cristo Rei on the far left

When you arrive at the ferry dock, turn left for Platform 20 where the bus departs. The journey time is around fifteen minutes. Tickets can be bought on board.

Santuário Nacional de Cristo Rei

The bus trundles through the town of **Almada** ❸ and up to the **Santuário Nacional de Cristo Rei** ❹ (National Sanctuary of Christ the King; www.cristorei.pt; charge for lift). The visitors here are a mix of Portuguese pilgrims paying their respects in the chapel of the Catholic Welcome Centre and tourists taking arms-outstretched selfies. Mass is held here every Sunday.

The tall, solitary statue stands proud at 110m (360ft), of which 82m (269ft) is pedestal and 28m (91ft) the robed figure blessing the city. Views from west to east embrace Belém, the Ponte 25 de Abril, downtown Lisbon, Castelo de São Jorge and the Vasco da Gama Bridge. On a clear day you can see as far as the Sierra of Sintra with the Palace of Pena on the hilltop.

Ponte 25 de Abril

The **Ponte 25 de Abril** ❺, which the statue overlooks, was also built under Portugal's long-time dictator, Salazar. Inspired by San Francisco's Golden Gate Bridge, it was originally called the Ponte Salazar but was renamed in honour of the bloodless revolution of 25 April 1974 that restored democracy to Portugal. In 1999 the lower tier of the bridge was adapted to accommodate a railway across the river. For those who don't mind heights, the Pilar 7 experience (Avenida da Índia 52; www.visitlisboa.com; charge), back on the Lisbon side of the river, affords views from an 80m-high glassed-in viewing platform. There's also an informative exhibition on the bridge's history.

For a good seafood lunch or dinner, head for **Atira-Te ao rio**, see ①, at Cais do Ginjal, about 1km (half a mile) west of the Cacilhas ferry stop.

Food and drink

① Atira-Te ao rio

Cais do Gingal 69/70, Almada; www.atirateaorio.pt; €€€
Enjoy stunning views of the city's skyline from the water's edge, while tucking into seafood from the simple menu. Shrimp soup or salad can be followed by a delicious *caldeirada de peixes e mariscos* (fish and seafood stew for two), or Portuguese favourite *bacalhau a lagareiro* (salted codfish in garlicky olive oil with roasted potatoes, punched and in their skin). If you are here in the early evening, come in time to watch the sun sink behind the Ponte 25 de Abril.

TOUR 9
Tram 28

Don't leave Lisbon without a trip on the city's vintage Tram No 28. Oozing tradition and charm, this little yellow gem rattles and lurches its way through the city's most picturesque and historic quarters.

DISTANCE: 7km (4.3 miles)
TIME: Approx 50 minutes (or longer depending on traffic)
START: Praça Martim Moniz; metro: Martim Moniz, green line
END: Estrela or Campo de Ourique (Prazeres)
POINTS TO NOTE: This is the most popular route in Lisbon and trams are usually packed with tourists. You can pick up the Tram No 28 in the Alfama, at the Sé (cathedral) or on Rua da Conceição in the Baixa but for the best chance of securing a seat, hop on at the starting point at Praça Martim Moniz. You can buy a ticket on board, though it works out cheaper if you use the rechargeable Via Viagem pre-paid ticket (see page 125), or you can use a Carris/metro pass. Trams run from 5.40am to around 10pm and depart roughly every ten minutes, less frequently in the early morning and late evening. Stops are indicated by large signs marked *paragem*. The tram is a favourite of pickpockets so keep a careful eye on valuables.

Lisbon has six tram lines. Those servicing Baixa and Belém are modernised and have sleek interiors, but the rest are pre-war. The system of electric tramways *(eléctricos)* started in 1901 and has been going strong ever since. These vintage trams, with their brightly painted yellow exteriors and wood-panelled interiors, are a nostalgic way to explore the city. The most famous and picturesque is No 28, which offers an excellent sightseeing tour of old Lisbon.

Don't take this route, however, if you are in a hurry. Just enjoy the ride and the opportunity to peer into tiny shady shop doorways, admire the pink clouds of geraniums spilling over wrought-iron balconies and catch the occasional glimpse of the river over the rooftops. Delays and crowds can mean a wait for a tram or one that you can find a space on, so this experience is one for an unhurried day.

As an alternative, Tram No 12 has a limited service, but tends to be slightly less crowded. It departs from Praça da Figueira,

The mustard-yellow trams are a defining part of Lisbon's cityscape

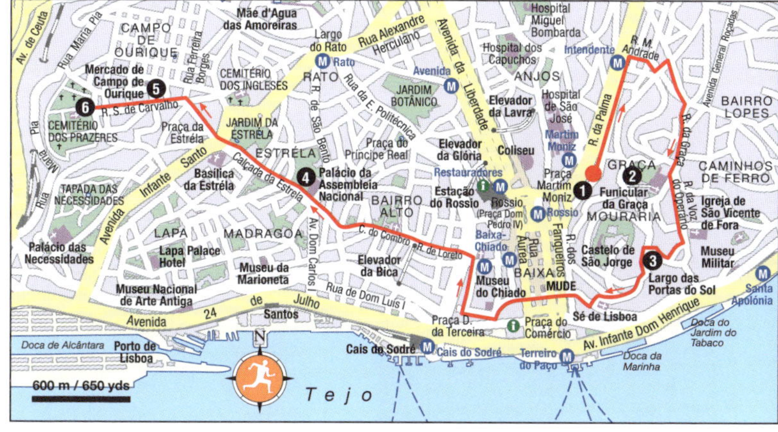

doing a picturesque loop around the castle and the Alfama.

Setting off

Catch Tram No 28 at **Praça Martim Moniz ❶**, ideally no later than 8am if you want to secure a seat. Grab a window seat if you can, preferably on the left-hand side for the best views. Although you may be tempted to hop off the tram mid-way, you would be lucky to find a seat on another No 28 (and that's not just in high season). To guarantee a space all the way, it's best to play safe and stay put. The tram will be marked Prazeres, and it heads north along the Avenida Almirante de Reis, passing through Indendente, now undergoing a dramatic revamp with an ever-growing crop of hip shops and cafés.

Graça and Alfama

The tram cranks up to the charming **Graça ❷** neighbourhood, clinging to the hill above the imposing church and monastery of São Vicente de Fora. It then stops at Largo da Graça, site of the conspicuous blue Vila Sousa, the village built by industrialists in the late nineteenth century for workers and their families. Passengers often alight here for the Miradouro da Graça, with an open-air café and great views of the castle and central Lisbon. It's particularly popular at sunset, with a glass in hand. Behind the *miradouro*, the Igreja da Graça dates to 1271 but underwent major reconstruction after the Great Earthquake.

The tram plunges down from Graça through the medieval streets of

Lisbon's vintage trams are a novel way to explore the city

The tram by Basílica da Estrela

picturesque Alfama. One of the busiest stops is the **Largo das Portas do Sol** ❸, with a beautiful view over the red rooftops to the River Tagus. This is the most convenient stop for the castle.

Baixa and Bairro Alto

From Largo das Portas do Sol, the tram rattles down to the Sé (Cathedral), trundles along the Rua da Conceição in the flat Baixa (lower town), then creaks its way up to the Largo do Chiado and its elegant stores and famous *A Brasiliera Café* just near the tram stop; next along is the nearby Praça Luís de Camões; then it's the picturesque Bairro Alto.

Estrela and Campo de Ourique

From Bairro Alto it's up and down long streets all the way to the smart district of Estrela, passing on the right the large **Palácio da Assembleia Nacional** ❹ (Parliament building; Praça da Constituição de 1976; www.parlamento.pt; charge, limited guided tours only) in the former São Bento Convent. Beyond, you are unlikely to miss the huge domed **Basílica da Estrela**, where the tram stops. Many tourists alight here as this is the last major tourist site along the route. After a visit to the church (see Walk 5), you can take a stroll in the delightful gardens opposite, where there is a café beside the pond.

Foodies should stay on the tram until at least the penultimate stop, Igreja Santo Condestável, for the **Mercado de Campo de Ourique** ❺ (Rua Coelho da Rocha), a nineteenth-century market with a great display of fresh produce and a hip food court with gourmet stalls serving everything from suckling pig to custard tarts and flavoured gins. It's open for brunch, lunch, snacks, dinner or evening drinks – often with music or entertainment.

The tram terminus is Prazeres, where you can visit the **Cemitério dos Prazeres** ❻, the huge Prazeres Cemetery, created in 1833 after the outbreak of a cholera epidemic. It has the graves and mausoleums of many famous Portuguese.

Cranking around the city

TOUR 10
Sintra

Known by the Romans as the Mountains of the Moon, the Serra da Sintra is a magical palace-dotted landscape which feels as if it has sprung from a storybook. If you choose just one trip from Lisbon, make it this one.

DISTANCE: 16km (10 miles)
TIME: 1 or 2 full days
START: Sintra railway station
END: Sintra
POINTS TO NOTE: Sintra is 26km (16 miles) northwest of Lisbon and is easily reached by train from Rossio Station (every 14–20 minutes, journey time 45 minutes). Trains are often very busy. Arrive early to avoid the crowds and head straight to Pena Palace (most tourists start in the centre and hit the palace later). The Scotturb Bus #434 (every 15 minutes from 9.15am) links the station, town centre, Pena Palace and Moorish Castle. Sintra is linked to the Quinta da Regaleira and Monseratte Palace by the less-frequent Scotturb Bus #435. Tickets, including day passes, can be bought online or from the bus driver. Pre-book palace tickets to guarantee entry. A good day to visit is a Monday, when Lisbon sights are closed but major ones in Sintra are open. Avoid Sundays, when palaces are free for Portuguese locals, thus crowded.

Draped across a cool fertile highland, Sintra was long the coveted summer retreat of Portuguese royalty. Praised by generations of travellers for the beauty of its forest glades and craggy mountains, enchanting views and eccentric buildings, the town is irresistible. Lord Byron, who could find little good to say about the Portuguese, was enamoured of Sintra and likened it to 'Elysium's gates'. The *Lawrence Hotel* where he began writing *Childe Harold's Pilgrimage* still stands and claims to be the oldest hotel on the Iberian peninsula.

Despite the daily influx of tourists, Sintra makes a romantic getaway. Clustered throughout the forested hillsides are old palaces and estates with spectacular vistas. Two peaks in the range are crowned by reminders of Sintra's past: Castelo dos Mouros, the ruins of a castle built by the Moors in the eighth century, and Palácio de Pena, the fantasy palace built by a German nobleman for his Portuguese queen. The views from either of these points stretch as far as the sea, and the entire area, thick with vegetation and paths through the hills, provides spectacular trekking.

Palácio da Pena

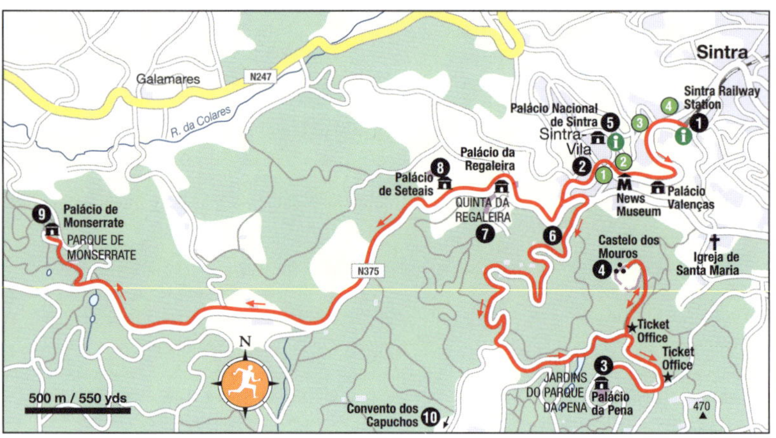

After Lisbon it seems like another world and has its own unique climate – a clash of warm southerlies and moist westerlies over the Serra da Sintra – and an almost bucolic way of life. In 1995 the Serra de Sintra was declared a UNESCO World Heritage Site. Ten national monuments are packed within the region's narrow boundaries. Ideally you should stay for two days or more, to see all the attractions.

Sintra is also accessible by car: take the IC-19 from Lisbon and follow signs for the centre when you arrive. However, note that roads in Sintra are very steep and narrow, there is a frustrating one-way system and parking is near impossible. Drivers should avoid rush-hour traffic and preferably weekends. If you're staying in Sintra in season it's easier to leave the car at your hotel and take the buses linking the main sights. If staying the night, see page 114 for accommodation.

Palácio da Pena

From **Sintra Railway Station** ❶ the Scotturb Bus #434 heads into the centre of Sintra, which is known as **Sintra-Vila** ❷, a picturesque small town with cobbled streets and tall, pastel-washed houses. It centres on the Palácio Nacional, distinguished from afar by its prominent twin conical chimneys. Stay on the bus, however, while it negotiates the hairpin bends through thick woods up to **Palácio da Pena** ❸ (Pena Palace; Estrada da Pena; www.parquesdesintra.pt; charge).

From the main entrance you can take the shuttle bus or walk by way of a park so lush with flowering trees and

The extraordinary design of Palácio da Pena

vines it resembles a tropical rainforest. On the highest peak of Sintra, 450m (1500ft) above sea level, the palace is visible from miles around. Close at hand, it is a bizarre and extravagant mishmash of Gothic, Renaissance, Moorish and Manueline architecture. The wild, layered facade is painted pink (the former monastery) and yellow (the new palace), framed by crenellated turrets, a studded archway and monsters guarding doorways. The views from the terraces sweep all the way from the Atlantic to Lisbon, best taken in from the alfresco café.

Palace interior

This fantastical castle of dreams was fashioned as a love nest for Maria II and her smitten husband, Prince Ferdinand of Saxe-Coburg-Gotha (cousin of Albert, consort to Queen Victoria). Few have had the wealth to indulge their free-running vision quite so grandly. Rooms are a swirling riot of imaginative, ornate and sumptuous detail. The original building was a Hieronymite monastery, built by Manuel I, severely damaged in the 1755 earthquake, but retaining the Manueline-style tiered cloister, decorated with patterned *azulejos*, and the beautiful tiled chapel.

The former monks' refectory became the dining room, and the monks' chapter house and dormitory the apartments of King Carlos. Rooms designed for the entertainment of VIP guests were the Arabic Room, with its mosque-like appearance and *trompe l'oeil* decoration, the lavishly decorated Great Hall and the Stag Room, styled in the fashion of a knights' banqueting hall, both rooms displaying wonderful stained glass – one of Ferdinand's great passions.

Palace grounds

To complete the hedonistic experience, strike out on a long stroll through the park, taking in the Valley of the Lakes, with a view of the palace stark against the sky, the Chalet and Garden of the Countess of Edla, the Garden of the Camellias and the Temple of Columns. Above, a marked footpath climbs up to the Cruz Alta (High Cross), which marks the highest point in the Sintra hills. (You will need the leaflet which comes with the ticket to find your way around.)

After the death of Queen Maria II during childbirth, Ferdinand married his mistress, Elise Hensler, a Swiss-American opera singer who had trained in Paris. She was later made Countess Edla, but her place within the Portuguese royal court was never fully accepted and Ferdinand chose not to cohabit with her in the palace itself. Instead, they built the **Chalet da Condessa d'Edla**, or 'House of Delights', a secluded idyllic retreat at the western end of the park. The couple created a romantic garden filled with an exotic collection of over two hundred

botanical species, among them camellias, azaleas, rhododendrons and tree ferns.

Castelo dos Mouros

Take the Vila Sassetti footpath (or bus) from the Pena Palace to the **Castelo dos Mouros** ❹ (www.parquesdesintra.pt; charge), the Moorish castle. Restored in the 1830s, this is the oldest monument in Sintra. The dauntless Dom Afonso Henrique seized it from the Moors in 1147, a major victory in the reconquest of Portugal. A fascinating ruin, its crenellated walls hug a rocky ridge overlooking the town. The highest peak (540m/1772ft) affords terrific views stretching to the sea and taking in the entire forested area, studded with secluded palaces and private *quintas* (estates). The mountainside is a luxuriant tangle of vegetation – subtropical plants, moss-choked boulders, giant ferns and walnut, chestnut and pine trees.

A delightful path zigzags its way down through the forest to Sintra-Vela via the Vila Sassetti garden – or you can use your bus ticket to return to town.

For sustenance in Sintra-Vela, try the pastries at **Casa Piriquita**, see ①, or the tapas at **Romaria de Baco**, see ②. Then make for the national palace, dominating the centre.

Palácio Nacional de Sintra

Distinctive for its twin chimneys, the **Palácio Nacional de Sintra** ❺ (National Palace; Largo Rainha Dona Amélia; www.parquesdesintra.pt; charge) lies in the heart of Sintra-Vela. The conspicuous chimneys were used to let the smoke out of the massive kitchen when oxen were being roasted in preparation for large banquets for visiting dignitaries.

A summer home for Portuguese kings since the early fourteenth century, the palace's design became more and more unpredictable and haphazard as wings were added over the centuries, with back-to-back medieval and Manueline styles. The interiors and furnishings are remarkable, peppered with exquisite antiques from all over the world and home to some of the oldest and most valuable collections of *azulejos* in Portugal. The grand abode continued as a residence for Portuguese royalty until the fall of the monarchy in 1910.

Palace interior

The so-called **Sala dos Cisnes** (Swan Room), used for banquets and receptions, was named after the ceiling panels, painted with 27 swans, all in different poses but each with a gold crown around its neck. Beyond, the **Sala das Pegas** (Magpie Salon), where notables were received, has a ceiling adorned with 136 magpies. King João I (1385–1433) had the panels painted after he was caught by Queen Philippa kissing one of her ladies-in-

Palácio Nacional de Sintra

waiting. Tongues furiously wagged until the king ordered the entire ceiling of the hall be painted with magpies – a barbed nod to the palace gossips. King Sebastião's room is hung with a portrait of the monarch who led a disastrous crusade to North Africa in 1578, the Battle of the Three Kings, when nearly 15,000 were captured or killed. The royal line was weakened and two years later, the Spanish annexed the Portuguese crown.

State rooms end with the striking **Sala das Basões**, its grand dome emblazoned with coats of arms of royalty and nobility, and the walls adorned with blue-and-white tiled panels depicting hunting and bucolic scenes. The prison room has a different tale to tell. The dull-witted Afonso VI (1643–1683) was pressured into abdicating to allow his more effective brother, Pedro II, to become king. When a plot to restore Afonso to the throne was discovered, the former monarch was exiled to Sintra and imprisoned in this simple room for nine years, until he died in 1683. The visit continues via the much-restored Palatine Chapel and culminates in the Arab Room with Moorish fountain and tiles.

If returning to Lisbon, it's only about a ten-minute walk to the station. Pop into **Fábrica das Verdadeiras**, see ❸, for pastries en route, or linger over a candlelit evening meal at **A Raposa**, see ❹, near the station.

Festival de Sintra

Sintra's lively summer festival (www.festivaldesintra.pt), held in May or June, features a series of musical events, mainly classical, which take place in historic palaces, estates and gardens in Sintra and the region.

Trains back to the capital run until after midnight (www.cp.pt).

Palácio Biester

On your second day in Sintra, a fifteen-minute walk uphill (2km/1.2 miles) or a short taxi ride or bus ride (#435) from the centre of Sintra will bring you to **Palácio Biester** ❻ (Avenida Almeida Garrett 1A; www.biester.pt; charge). Constructed in the late nineteenth century, in the heart of lush Biester Park, the palace only opened to the public in 2022. Without the overwhelming fame of its neighbours, it generally remains blissfully uncrowded in comparison to its counterparts. Spend a serene hour or two here to learn more about the history of Portugal's Knight Templars in the basement's Initiation Chamber, before admiring the ornately frescoed chapel and wonderfully embellished wood-carved ceilings in the music and living halls.

Quinta da Regaleira

Continue a few minutes along the road to reach **Quinta da Regaleira** ❼

The Swan Room's ceiling

Quinta da Regaleira's 'initiation well'

(Rua Barbosa du Bocage 5; www.regaleira.pt; charge), one of Sintra's oldest and grandest *quintas*. This fantastic late nineteenth-century multi-turreted mansion has magical and mysterious gardens speckled with follies such as the 'initiation well' accessed via a spiralling staircase. The palace interior was designed by an Italian theatre set designer and architect, Luigi Manini, for millionaire Brazilian merchant Antonio Carvalho Monteiro and his family. The exuberant mix of Manueline, Gothic and Renaissance styles would be out of place anywhere but Sintra, but it is the gardens that are the main calling card with their grottos, underground walkways, fountains and a Promenade of the Gods, flanked by statues of nine classical gods.

Palácio de Seteais

Just along the road on the other side is the **Palácio de Seteais** ❽ (Rua Barbosa du Bocage 8; www.tivolihotels.com). *Seteais* means 'seven sighs', clearly a nod to the great beauty of the surroundings. The palace was turned into a luxury hotel and restaurant in 1955 but many of its original features have been preserved; it is worth seeing, if only for tea or a drink. Grand rooms are decorated with crystal chandeliers, tapestries, murals and antique furnishings. From the gardens, with sculpted hedges and lemon trees, are magnificent views of the countryside – inspiration for Byron, no less.

Palácio de Monserrate

Another 2.5km (1.5 miles) along the wooded road will bring you to **Palácio de Monserrate** ❾ (Rua Barbosa du Bocage 136; www.parquesdesintra.pt; charge). Take the #435 bus or order a taxi at the hotel. This Moorish-style villa, inspired by Brighton Pavilion, was built in the nineteenth century and set among exotic lush gardens. After Pena Palace with all its crowds, peaceful Monserrate is a delight to visit. The first palace was built by Gerard de Visme, an English merchant, in 1790. The hugely wealthy English novelist, art collector and politician, William Beckford, fell in love with it and rented the palace from 1793 until 1799, restoring the property and constructing its first botanical garden. Half a century later, English textile merchant and art collector Sir Francis Cook bought the property, turned it into a romantic Moorish/Gothic folly and, with help from the head gardener of Kew Gardens, landscaped the grounds.

Lord Byron was inspired by a visit to Monserrate in 1809 and praises its beauty in *Childe Harold*. After this it became compulsory viewing for writers and artists, especially English ones, on their travels to Portugal. The gardens have a remarkable collection of species from five continents, from ornamental

Palácio de Monserrate

lakes, waterfalls and fountains to tree ferns and palm-trees; agaves and yuccas recreate a corner of Mexico. The palace, recently restored and reopened, reflects the eclectic spirit of the nineteenth century, with its Moorish-Gothic and Italian-style influences.

Convento dos Capuchos

If you have a car, don't miss a visit to one of the strangest sights of the Serra: the **Convento dos Capuchos** ⑩ (Estrada dos Capuchos; 3.6km (2 miles) on the N375 from the Palácio de Monserrate or 8km (5 miles) from Sintra along the N247; www.parquesdesintra.pt; charge), an atmospheric Franciscan monastery tucked away in the woods and built entirely out of rocks and cork. There are no buses, but you can walk to the monastery from Sintra, along a wooded road, or take a taxi for around €40 return.

It was built in the sixteenth century but abandoned in 1834 with the suppression of the religious orders in Portugal. Small, simple and rustic, it is almost completely swallowed up by its rural surrounds, to the extent that granite boulders have been incorporated into the building. A few cells are so tiny you have to crawl through. Some say the monks lined them with cork to obtain absolute silence – but there is little noise in the forest other than birdsong. More likely, the material helped the residents tolerate the long and humid winters.

Praia de Maçãs

After a visit in 1581, King Philip I of Portugal (also Philip II of Spain) stated that in all his kingdoms, the two places he most preferred were El Escorial (in Spain) for its wealth and the Capuchos Convent in Sintra for its poverty.

Beaches

The proximity of good beaches is yet another attraction of Sintra, as is the enjoyable ride on the quaint tram that trundles to the coast all year (three a day in season, two in winter but no trains in November). The tram spits passengers out at **Praia das Maçãs**, liveliest of the resorts on this coast, packed with seafood restaurants. The tram twists, bumps and screeches its way through some lovely scenery.

Monserrate's interior

Medieval cloister of the Convento dos Capuchos

Food and drink

1 Casa Piriquita
Rua das Padarias 1; www.piriquita.pt; €
Opposite the National Palace in the town centre, this would be an inconspicuous café were it not for the long queues outside clamouring to buy its famous tarts. It is noisy, friendly and packed with Portuguese, but worth the wait for a table or a chance to buy from the bakery. Since 1862, it has been producing scrumptious little *queijadas* (sweet cheese pastries that were used as a form of payment in medieval times) and *travesseiros* ('pillows', with a creamy almond filling). There's a second branch up the road, at Rua das Padarias 18.

2 Romaria de Baco
Rua Gil Vicente 2;
www.romariadebaco.pt; €€
Just off the main square, this informal restaurant has a good range of tapas and *petiscos* (snacks), as well as vegetarian dishes, salads and Portuguese meat and fish specials.

3 Fábrica das Verdadeiras (Queijadas da Sapa)
Volta do Duche 12;
www.facebook.com/queijadasdasapa; €
On the road between the station and the centre, and announced by a mouthwatering aroma, this *fábrica* has been churning out *queijadás de Sintra* (pastries with a filling of cottage cheese, egg and sugar) for over 150 years. Try them with coffee, or perhaps a glass of port, in this small, welcoming café or take them away in packs of six.

4 A Raposa
Rua Conde Ferreira 29;
www.restaurantearaposa-sintra.com; €€€
On a side street near the station, this daytime café and evening restaurant set in the dining room of a charming old house offers delicious Portuguese and Mediterranean dishes. The bread is home-made and served warm with fresh local cheese and olive oil. Impromptu *fado* may be thrown in.

If you have a car, head for the less touristy **Praia Grande** to the south, a broad sandy beach where you can enjoy gorgeous sea and sunset views at *Bar do Fundo*, maybe with sushi or sea bass, washed down with *vinho verde*. Or there is lovely little **Adraga**, with soft sand, rock formations and another excellent fish restaurant. Beware, though, this is the Atlantic and both beaches are pounded by ferocious rollers. North of Praia das Maçãs, **Azenhas do Mar** is a lovely village clinging to the cliff face, with a small beach and natural rock seawater pools for swimming.

The village of Azenhas do Mar

TOUR 11
The Cascais coast

Take a trip to Lisbon's illustrious beach resorts, whose balmy climate and gracious lifestyle lured exiled royalty, nobility and spies in the past century. In summer Lisboetas escape the steamy city for the cooler Atlantic shores.

DISTANCE: Train Lisbon to Estoril 26km (16 miles); walk Estoril and Cascais 4km (2.5 miles); cycle to Praia do Guincho 9km (5.5 miles); drive Lisbon to Cabo da Roca 50km (31 miles).
TIME: A full day
START: Cais do Sodré, Lisbon
END: Cabo do Roca (or Cascais)
POINTS TO NOTE: Estoril and Cascais are linked to Lisbon by regular trains from Cais do Sodré (30–45 minutes). Depending on time you could skip Estoril – Cascais has more attractions. A great way to reach the Guincho beaches from Cascais is to bike along the coastal cycle path. Cheap, basic bikes (*bicas*) can be picked up opposite the Cascais train station or you can hire rides (including e-bikes) from Tomorrow's Adventure (www.tomorrowsadventure.pt), inside the station. Buses connect Cascais with Praia do Guincho and Cabo da Roca (different routes), though services are not regular enough to depend on.

West of Lisbon, and easily reached by train, this cosmopolitan playground offers first-rate hotels and restaurants, a glorious coastline, excellent sporting facilities and a history, culture and atmosphere quite unlike that of Lisbon. Beaches are very much part of the attraction, from the sands of Cascais and Estoril, teeming in high season, to the less-crowded Atlantic-battered beaches further north. Cascais and Estoril both make excellent bases from which to explore the coastline. Hire a car for the most flexibility and easy access to Cabo da Roca. If this is your preference, note that renting a vehicle in Cascais removes the stress of contending with Lisbon traffic.

Estoril

Take the Cascais train from Cais do Sodré, with views of the Tagus and the Atlantic, and alight at **Estoril**. As early as the mid-eighteenth century, this coastal town was luring visitors to its climate and thermal spa baths. During World War II the area acquired a glamorous reputation, attracting a

Praia dos Pescadores, the main beach in Cascais

wave of royal refugees, among them the toppled King Umberto II of Italy, Carol II of Romania, Miklós Horthy, Regent of Hungary and Don Juan (father of Juan Carlos I of Spain).

Enjoying the breeze of neutral Portugal, German spies flocked to the *Hotel Parque* (torn down after the war), while their English counterparts lodged at the grander *Palácio Estoril* (still standing). Ian Fleming was reputedly inspired to write his first James Bond novel, *Casino Royale*, after his stay here, and the hotel served as a backdrop for scenes in the 1969 film, *On Her Majesty's Secret Service*.

Estoril today is both a tourist and business resort and a place for summer homes and comfortable retirement. It may not be as grand as it used to be, but it retains a certain elegance and sophistication, has gardens of palms and pines, golden (but crowded) sands and world-class golf courses.

Casino Estoril

The train station is conveniently located between the main attractions: the beach of Tamariz and the formal gardens stretching up to the modern **casino** ❶ (Praça José Teodoro dos Santos; www.casino-estoril.pt; ID required, gamblers must be 18 or over, no shorts, sportswear or sandals). Europe's second-largest casino, this is Estoril's one-stop after-dark hangout with its nightclub, restaurants, bars, cinema, exhibition halls, shops, shows and entertainment. Gambling is suspended on only two nights a year: Good Friday and Christmas Eve. Legend has it that somebody broke the bank one Good Friday, prompting a superstitious management to declare

Family-friendly Praia do Tamariz

Arneiro
Queluz
Sintra
Alcabideche
PARQUE URBANO PENHAS DA MARMELEIRA
Hospital de Cascais dr. José de Almeida
A16
9-1
6-8
A5
Murches
Aldeia de Juzo
Bairro de Alegria
Quinta Patino
Quinta Pedagógica Armando Villar
593
Alvide
São Gabriel
Pai do Vento
Amoreira
Bairro de São José
Estoril Palácio Golf Course
Lisboa
597
Birre
Cobre
Bairro Mal. Carmona
Fontainhas
Bairro de Pampilheria
Alto da Pampilheria
Quinta da Bicuda
Monte Estoril
Casino Estoril
Igreja de Santo António do Estoril
Torre
Bairro da Assunção
Estoril
Oeiras
Bairro do Rosário
Promenade
Praia do Tamariz
Praia das Moitas
Praia da Duquesa
Cascais
Praia da Conceição
Praia da Rainha
Guia
Ermida de Nossa Senhora da Guia
Museu do Mar
Praia dos Pescadores
Baia de Cascais
Casa das Histórias Paula Rego
247
Farol da Guia
Gandarinha
Museu Condes de Castro Guimarães
Cidadela and Pousada
Marina de Cascais
Boca do Inferno
Farol Museum de Santa Marta
Praia de Santa Marta
ATLÂNTICO

it a holiday thenceforth; officials dismiss the story as wishful thinking.

Praia do Tamariz

Just below the bus and train stations the **Praia do Tamariz** ❷ (Tamariz Beach) buzzes all summer. With its relatively calm seas and plentiful facilities, including a string of lively bars and restaurants, it's a popular spot for Portuguese families and holiday camps. There are a few outfits renting loungers

Casino Estoril

Cascais's town square with Dom Pedro statue

and parasols, including a 'pool' area on the sands complete with drinks service.

From Estoril you can walk to neighbouring Cascais along the attractive seaside **promenade** ❸ (fifteen minutes), popular with local joggers, cyclists and strollers. Cafés along the way frame fine sea views.

Cascais

Known as the town of kings and fishermen, it was here that King Luís I (1838–1889) established his summer residence in the sea-view citadel. And it was in Cascais that the royal family first acquired the habit of taking to the beach and bathing – not just for fun but for therapeutic and medicinal purposes. The aristocracy from all over Portugal followed suit, building palaces and stately mansions, turning Cascais into a cosmopolitan resort. After the assassination of King Carlos in 1908 and the proclamation of the Republic two years later, Cascais was left in the hands of the fisherfolk – but not for long. In 1926, when the railway link from Lisbon became electrified, it was already becoming a seaside paradise with its golden sands, fine scenery and seafood restaurants.

Cascais is now a large and vibrant resort, retaining some elegant nineteenth-century villas along the coastline, good beaches and an attractive old quarter, albeit very tourist-orientated. Fishing as an industry has almost died out, though there are vestiges of the old fishing village and lobster pots piled high beside the main Praia dos Pescadores.

The town centre

The town centre has prettily cobbled pedestrian streets with cafés, restaurants and pubs spilling out on to the pavement and buzzing late into the night. The main focus is the Largo Luís de Camões. The alfresco cafés here have their charm, but for something less touristy, head north to the revamped market and join the Portuguese at **Marisco Na Praça**, see ①, for arguably the best fish in town. For sea views choose **Baía do Peixe**, see ②, or for bargain spicy grilled chicken and chips, **Somos um Regalo**, see ③, is a five-minute walk west of Largo Luís de Camões.

Praia dos Pescadores

Cidadela

The cultural attractions of Cascais are all to the west of the centre. Overlooking the bay is the **Cidadela** ❹, a seventeenth-century military fort and one of the few buildings to have survived the earthquake and tidal wave of 1755. It has been restored and is now home to a modern pousada, which manages the stylish art studios and galleries around the square, and a *taberna* serving tapas and Portuguese pastries on the square in summer. The yellow building overlooking the square is the summer residence of the Portuguese president. On the far side of the citadel is the swish **marina**, flanked by fancy bars, restaurants and shops.

Parque Municipal

West of the citadel is the **Parque Municipal**, a well-kept park with tropical vegetation, fountains, statues and peacocks. Overlooking a small creek, within a castle-like turreted mansion, is the **Museu Condes de Castro Guimarães** ❺ (Avenida Rei Humberto Ii de Itália; www.bairrodosmuseus.cascais.pt; charge). This was the home of the Count of Guimarães who bequeathed the mansion, along with all its antiques, paintings and porcelain, to the town in 1892.

Casa das Histórias Paula Rego

A brief walk takes you to **Casa das Histórias Paula Rego** ❻ (House of Stories Paula Rego; Avenida da República; www.fundacaodomluis.pt; charge). The museum makes a bold statement with its two terracotta towers, inspired by the chimney towers of Sintra's National Palace. It is dedicated to the Portuguese-born, London-based Paula Rego, Portugal's most famous female artist. The collection showcases her (often unsettling) paintings, drawings and etchings – many reflecting issues related to feminism and the patriarchy – over fifty years of her prolific career.

Museu do Mar

Just to the east is the **Museu do Mar** ❼ (Maritime Museum; Rua Júlio Pereira de Mello; www.bairrodosmuseus.cascais.pt; charge), which captures much of the town's fishing heritage and displays treasure recovered from

Estoril Music Festival

The long-established Estoril Music Festival (www.festorilisbon.com) platforms some of the world's most prestigious chamber orchestras and soloists, but also opens the stage to young talent from across the world. The event takes place over three weeks in July and concerts are held in the Estoril Congress Centre, the Cascais Cultural Centre, Monastery of Jerónimos in Belém and other prestigious settings in Lisbon.

Peacock in the park

Casa das Histórias Paula Rego

Sports galore

Sports enthusiasts are spoilt for choice on the Cascais coast. Top surfers come for the Atlantic rollers north of Cascais; kayaking, bodyboarding, kitesurfing and waterskiing are also popular. Estoril is a well-known all-year golf resort with several courses in the surrounding area. Some hotels offer special golf holiday deals. The luxurious Palácio Estoril (see page 115) owns the famous Golf do Estoril, designed by Mckenzie Ross. Some of the most important golf tournaments have taken place here.

sunken wrecks. This is the site of the old Sporting Club of Cascais, founded by King Carlos, where the leisured classes came for croquet, target shooting, scavenger hunts, lawn tennis matches and football (the first match in Portugal was played here in 1888).

East of the museum is a peaceful old quarter with pretty streets around the **Igreja de Nossa Senhora da Assuncão**. The plain facade of the church belies a feast of gilt and pre-earthquake *azulejos* inside.

Praia do Guincho

A short drive or bracing fifteen-minute walk west along the seafront from Cascais will bring you to the **Boca do Inferno** ❽ (Mouth of Hell), a geological curiosity where in rough weather the waves send up fierce fountains of spray, accompanied by ferocious sound effects. Another good reason for visiting is the **Mar do Inferno**, see ❹, with its superb seafood. In another 2.5km (1.5 miles) there is another shellfish haven: the **Furnas do Guincho**, see ❺.

The N247 coastal road wiggles north to **Praia do Guincho** ❾, a spectacular sweeping beach where foam-tipped rollers crash onto the sands. It is a mecca for professional surfers and windsurfers, hosting the Portuguese National Surfing and Body Boarding Championships. Surf shops rent out gear, including wetsuits which are recommended even in summer. Strong swells form dangerous riptides, and the waves here are not for beginners or weak swimmers. Set on the rocks, with spectacular views of the ocean, is the five-star **Hotel Fortaleza do Guincho**, a former fort which shelters a Michelin-starred restaurant (see page 121).

Cabo da Roca

The coast road climbs over craggy cliffs as far as windswept **Cabo da Roca** (13km/8 miles), where cliffs plunge into the sea. For a fee, the tourist office here will provide you with a certificate (in antique or modern style) confirming you have reached the most westerly point of mainland Europe. A lighthouse sits at the top of the cliffs at 140m (459ft). Beware of strong gusts of wind.

Surfers at Praia do Guincho

Food and drink

① Marisco Na Praça

Mercado da Vila, Cascais; www.mariscoanapraca.com; €€€

You won't get fish much fresher than at *Marisco Na Praça*, set in the newer market right next door to the fish stalls and with a magnificent array of seafood to select from. Price is by the kilo or 100g so take care when choosing so that you have a rough idea of the cost – and note the bread and olives on the table don't come free of charge. Choose from red king prawns, razor clams, sea bass, king crabs – and plenty more. Reservations advisable.

② Baía do Peixe

Avenida Dom Carlos 1, Cascais; www.baiadopeixe.com; €€€

This inviting fish restaurant above the Praia das Pescadores has lovely bay views from the terrace. There's a fair-priced lunch special, but the main draw are the magnificent stacked and refillable seafood platters (for a minimum of two people), which are well worth the splurge.

③ Somos um Regalo

Avenida Vasco da Gama 36, Cascais; tel: 214-865 487; €

This simple *churrasqueira* is known for its *franguinho da Guia*, chicken served as spicy as you like it, barbecued to a tasty crisp, served with tomato salad, rice and chips, and washed down with sangria or a cheap glass of wine. Good pastries too. Takeaway also available. Expect to queue.

④ Mar do Inferno

Boca do Inferno, Avenida Rei Humberto II Itália, Cascais; www.mardoinferno.pt; €€€

This long-established family-run haunt sits on the cliffs north of Cascais and offers a fabulous choice of fresh fish and seafood. Take your pick from cataplana clams, goose barnacles (tastier than they look), sea bream, sole or large Cascais crab. Excellent wines, too – ask the staff for recommendations. Booking advisable.

⑤ Furnas do Guincho

Estrada do Guincho, www.furnasdoguincho.pt; €€€€

Watch Atlantic waves crash against the coast while tucking into stuffed spider crab, rock lobster, shellfish paella, fish stew Furnas-style or whole seabass baked in a salt crust. Booking is essential at this buzzing modern restaurant with its seductive setting on the rocks.

If driving, return to Lisbon via the coastal road ('the Marginal') or, for more excitement, try your luck at the casino in Estoril (maybe with a Chinese meal at its excellent *Mandarim* restaurant) or party the night away in Cascais.

Lighthouse at Cabo da Roca

TOUR 12
Serra da Arrábida

A car is essential for this trip to the spectacular and unspoiled Serra da Arrábida. The tour starts at the fishing port of Setúbal, renowned for fish restaurants, then takes in glorious beaches and rugged green hills before heading west to Sesimbra and the windswept promontory of Cabo Espichel.

DISTANCE: 185km (115.5 miles) including return journey from Lisbon
TIME: One or two full days
START: Setúbal
END: Cabo Espichel
POINTS TO NOTE: From Lisbon you can cross the Tagus by either bridge: the Ponte Vasco da Gama (A12) or the Ponte 25 de Abril (A2), depending on your starting point. The latter is slightly shorter in distance but often takes longer due to traffic. Both are subject to tolls. To return to Lisbon from Cabo Espichel, take the A2. Tours of the Palácio and Quinta da Bacalhõa must be booked in advance. For the José Maria da Fonseca Winery you can usually just turn up and join a tour, but a reservation is worthwhile to be on the safe side.

The star attraction of the peninsula is the **Parque Natural de Arrábida**, a protected national park with a 22 mile (35km) -long mountain chain that protects the coast from the strong north winds and is rich in Mediterranean vegetation. The landscape is wonderfully rugged: wild green slopes stark against the intense blue sea. On the southern side the waves have nibbled away at the hills, sculpting the coastline into towering craggy cliffs and hidden sandy beaches. On the northern side are vine-combed hills.

Setúbal

Although **Setúbal** ❶ is an industrial city and the third-largest fishing port in Portugal, it preserves a pedestrianised historic centre, a wealth of seafood restaurants and one of the finest fish markets in the country. The region also produces the highly regarded sweet Moscatel de Setúbal wines.

The fishing industry goes back centuries. If you visit the tourist office at Travessa Frei Gaspar 10, a glass floor reveals the remains of Roman tanks from a factory where fish was salted and processed into sauces *(garum)* and condiments. These were packed

The Convento da Arrábida dates back to the sixteenth century

in amphorae and exported by sea, mainly to Rome. In the early twentieth century Setúbal was Portugal's number one centre for sardines. A more recent claim to fame is as the birthplace of national hero José Mourinho.

Convento de Jesus

North of the tourist office, attractive narrow streets spiral through the old town, leading off the jacaranda-shaded Largo da Misericordia. The cultural big-hitter is the **Convento de Jesus** (Largo Jesus; www.mun-setubal.pt; charge), a glorious church whose high-arched ceiling is supported by six great twisted pillars; walls are decorated with fine *azulejo* panels. One of the first examples of Manueline architecture, it was built in 1490 by the architect who later created Lisbon's famous Jerónimos Monastery. The adjoining monastery was converted into the **Museu de Setúbal**, home to a fine collection of sixteenth-century Portuguese and Flemish paintings, sacred gold and silver plates, archaeological finds and *azulejos*. At the east end of the city, you can see displays of salting, canning and agriculture at the **Museo de Trabalho** (Largo Defensores da República; www.mun-setubal.pt; charge). The canneries may have closed but Setúbal is still renowned for fresh fish, so head down to the port and choose from the restaurants for the catch of the day. **O Miguel**, see ①, is a good bet.

On the south side of the Avenida Luísa Todi, the **Mercado do Livramento** (Tues–Sun 7.30am–2pm) is a splendid market building decorated with striking *azulejos*. It has dazzling

Palmela

On a spur of the wooded Serra da Arrabida, north of Setúbal, unfolds the attractive little hill town of Palmela. It centres around a medieval castle whose terraces offer spectacular views over the peninsula, the Sado estuary and, on a clear day, as far as Lisbon to the north. Originally a Moorish stronghold, the castle was later expanded to incorporate a monastery. After painstaking restoration it was converted into one of Portugal's finest pousadas (see page 115). Palmela is a viticultural centre and the town hosts an annual wine festival, the Festa das Vindimas, on the first weekend of September.

displays of fruit and vegetables, cheeses, hams and gleaming fresh fish, including whole tuna and swordfish.

Sado Estuary

In summer regular ferries ply the waters between Setúbal and the **Tróia Peninsula** ❷, a long, sandy spit jutting out into the Sado estuary threaded with popular Atlantic-facing white beaches. It is home to the luxury *Tróia Resort*, a 1200-acre sprawl of tower blocks, but you can find dense forest, pristine beaches and untamed dunes further south. Tróia is said to be the site of the Roman town of Cetóbriga, destroyed by a tidal wave in the fifth century. The Roman ruins of a fish-salting centre are open to the public. The wild **Estuário do Sado** ❸ is a haven for waders, including the black-winged stilt, sandpipers and spoonbills in spring and summer, and avocets, flamingos, cormorants, herons and plovers come winter. The water is also home to a permanent colony of bottlenose dolphins, with regular **whalewatching trips** departing from Setúbal and Troía in season. The playful creatures often swim alongside the boats.

Arrábida beaches

Take the coast road west out of Setúbal and wind your way up through woodland of pines, palms and cypresses (try to ignore the cement factory at Outão – the only eyesore that mars the natural beauty). Just below the road are some fabulous beaches. Beware, though – these are popular (particularly **Figueirinha**, nearest to Setúbal) and parking in summer can be impossible unless you arrive early. Try secluded **Galapos**, which has trickier access, hence gloriously fewer visitors. The sea is a kaleidoscope of blues and greens – ideal for snorkelling. The last of the beaches, **Portinho da Arrábida** ❹ is a beautiful bathing spot laced by white sand. Grilled fish is the order of the day at its sleepy waterside restaurants.

Estrada de Escarpa

Shortly after Portinho da Arrábida, take the right (N379) signposted

Praça do Bocage, Setúbal

Convento da Arrábida ❺ (Rua São Lourenço; www.foriente.pt/a-fundacao/convento-arrabida; charge). High above the beaches, the sixteenth-century Franciscan monastery was resurrected as part of Lisbon University. It enjoys fine views of the coast and has five small chapels tucked into the folds of the hills where the monks sought solitude. A path from the convent leads to the summit of **Formosinho**, the highest point of the Serra da Arrábida (500m); expansive vistas reward those who embark on the challenging hike (2hr). Visits are only possible on Wednesdays, Saturdays and Sundays and require reservations.

From the monastery the road climbs steeply up the serra, with sensational views as you drop down the Tróia peninsula and Rio Sado. At Outão, turn left and wind across the mountains to Vila Fresca Azeitão.

Azeitão

A cluster of small *aldeias* or villages, prosperous **Azeitão** is known for red wine, olives and creamy sheep's cheese. The olive groves gave the region the name of Azeitão, meaning 'large olive tree'. From Vila Fresca de Azeitão, follow signs for **Vila Nogueira de Azeitão** ❻. The villages are also known for patisserie, so recharge the batteries with a *bica* (espresso) and the famous *torta de Azeitão*, a soft sponge roll filled with egg, cream and cinnamon. Try the café opposite the **Casa Museu José Maria de Fonseca** (see below); it also sells the delicious Azeitão cheese, an unpasteurised sheep's milk cheese produced in small rounds. It is still churned out by a few families in artisan dairies. If it's time for lunch, try **Casa das Tortas**, see ❷, on the Praça da República.

Wineries

Large black barrels in the centre of town herald the wine cellars of the famous José Maria da Fonseca Winery, founded in 1834. The winery today remains a family business (now in its seventh generation) and produces the soft, rich Periquita, Portugal's oldest table wine – as well as Setúbal's popular dessert Moscatel wines. The main building of the winery is a nineteenth-century mansion, which was the Fonseca family residence. The **Casa Museu José Maria da Fonseca** (Rua José Augusto Coelho, www.jmf.pt; charge) has guided tours in English, French and Spanish as well as Portuguese, which include a visit to the Moscatel cellar, whose hallowed vault stores bottles that are over a hundred years old. You won't be tasting these particular vintages, but you will have the chance to sample red Fonseca wine and 20-year-old Moscatel. Should you miss out on a tour you can try before you buy at the **Loja de Vinhos**, the large wine shop which has longer opening hours and tastings.

Just over 2km (1.25km) northeast on the N10, the **Bacalhôa Vinhos**

The hill town of Palmela

Postcard-pretty Azeitão

de Portugal ❼ (www.bacalhoa.pt; charge) is one of the biggest wineries in Portugal, producing reds, whites, rosés and sparkling wines. A visit here is about art as much as grapes, with a museum showcasing stunning exhibitions of African art, Art Nouveau and Art Deco contemporary sculpture. The **palácio** (pre-booked guided tours available) was built in 1480 and its architecture, decor and gardens reflect the tastes of various owners over the years who drew inspiration from their travels across Europe, Africa and Asia. There are beautiful *majolica azulejos* from the sixteenth century, including *Susanna and the Elders* (1565) in the lakehouse, the earliest known panel in Portugal.

Sesimbra

Sixteen kilometres (10 miles) westwards along the N379 brings you to **Sesimbra** ❽, a bustling fishing port and beach resort. Locals flock here at weekends and holidays for superb seafood, hedonistic nights and the sandy beach, sheltered (in summer at least) from the brunt of Atlantic tides and harsh winds.

The beach is divided into two by the restored seventeenth-century **Fortaleza de Santiago**, home to the tourist office and the **Museu Maritimo** (Rua da Fortaleza 27; www.visitsesimbra.pt; charge), dedicated to local fishing traditions through the centuries. There's also a restaurant within the fort overlooking the ocean; outside of meal service times, it's possible to take in the views with a drink.

The catch of the day is served in the many excellent seafood restaurants, including **Casa Mateus**, see ❸, just inland. A favoured local dish of Sesimbra is *arroz de marisco*, a shellfish and rice plate that is ideal for sharing. Another speciality is black scabbard, celebrated for ten days in May/June during the Black Scabbard Fish Gastronomic Week; the spotlight swivels to the humble swordfish in September for a week-long culinary event.

The local fishing boats set out from the **Porto di Abrigo** at the far western end of town and bring home their daily catch to be auctioned to restaurateurs. Visitors can join a guided tour to the fish auction on Tuesdays and Thursday afternoons (book at the tourist office), though there is nothing to stop you going independently.

It's a noisy and absorbing affair, with the fish announced through loudspeakers while buyers and spectators look on from rows of tiered seats, watching the large trays of glistening fish on the conveyor belts below.

Castelo de Sesimbra

Silhouetted on the hilltop above Sesimbra and signed from the main road is the restored **Castelo de Sesimbra** ❾ (Rua Nossa Sra. do Castelo 11; www.visitsesimbra.pt; free). During

Wine barrels decorated with antique *azulejos*, Bacalhôa Vinhos de Portugal

the Middle Ages the town was located here, protected against sea raiders by its walls and altitude. The Moors built the enclave, lost it to King Afonso Henriques in 1165, and seized it back again for a few years before having to move out permanently in 1200.

Peer inside the **Church of Our Lady of the Consolation of the Castle** within the outer fortifications. It was rebuilt during the eighteenth century and the walls are covered in *azulejos* from floor to ceiling.

The view down to the curve of the coast and back to the Arrábida mountains is magnificent.

Cabo Espichel

The Arrábida peninsula ends dramatically with the cliffs of **Cabo Espichel** ⑩, 11km (7 miles) west of Sesimbra. This wind-pummelled promontory with its lighthouse and stunning sea views is also the site of the seventeenth-century sanctuary of **Nossa Senhora do Cabo**, decorated with a *trompe l'oeil* ceiling, Baroque paintings and decorative tiles. Sadly, it's closed more often than not.

This used to be an important pilgrimage site, and you can still see the two rows of pilgrims' lodgings, now blocked up, forming two sides of a courtyard.

From Cabo Espichel, it's approximately a 50km (31 miles) drive back to Lisbon, via the A2 and the Ponte 25 de Abril.

Food and drink

① O Miguel

Avenida José Mourinho 16, Setúbal; www.omiguel.pt; €€€

Setúbal has plenty of good fish restaurants and this one, by the fishing harbour, ranks among the best. Try *dourada* (gilt-head bream), *robalo* (seabass) or *chocos fritos* (deep-fried cuttlefish), washed down with very affordable Setúbal wines. Formerly the Rua da Saude, this street has been named after the football manager who was born in Setúbal.

② Casa das Tortas

Praça da Republica 37, Vila Nogueira de Azeitão; tel: 969-146 996; €€

Come for simply grilled fish and meat dishes and stay for speciality *tortas* (cakes) from Azeitão with a glass of local *moscatel*. In summer, sit at trestle tables on the tree-shaded terrace. Good value.

③ Casa Mateus

Largo Anselmo Braancamp 4, Sesimbra; www.casamateus.pt; €€€

This small, sought-after seafood restaurant, near the fort, has been in the same family for nearly a hundred years. Pick from cuttlefish, seafood curry, fish stew or grouper with clams, and leave room for dessert. Excellent service. Reservations advisable.

Crowds packing out Sesimbra's beach

TOUR 13
Mafra and Ericeira

A fascinating trip from Lisbon, either by bus or car, this tour takes in the monumental Palace-Convent of Mafra, designated a UNESCO World Heritage Site in 2019, and a visit to Ericeira, superb for seafood and surf beaches and with a delightful fishing village at its core.

DISTANCE: Lisbon to Mafra 44km (27.5 miles), Mafra to Ericeira 10km (6 miles)
TIME: Full day
START: Lisbon
END: Ericeira
POINTS TO NOTE: A car affords more flexibility for this route, but you can also travel by bus (40min or 90min). The service, operated by Carris Metropolitana (www.carrismetropolitana.pt), departs from Lisbon's Campo Grande terminal (served by Campo Grande Metro station). Buses marked 'Ericeira via Mafra' depart at least once an hour, more in peak season. Payment methods and cards are the same as in Lisbon. The bus stops in front of Mafra National Palace; some continue to Ericeira. By car, the quickest route to Mafra is north along the A8; at junction 5, turn off west onto the A21 (signed Malveira/Mafra/Ericeira), taking exit 3 for the palace. Both are toll roads, but the journey is only about half an hour.

Mafra is a name shared by both a small modest town and a grandiose palace-convent of staggering dimensions. The facade of the latter, which is often likened to El Escorial in Spain, measures over 220m (726ft), and the royal gallery, stretching 232m, is the largest palace corridor in Europe. The eighteenth-century architectural masterpiece was created by João V to celebrate the awaited birth of his first child, Princess Dona Maria. When originally built it was intended as a modest Franciscan monastery, but it soon morphed into a lavish palace and basilica. Such magnificence was possible due to the influx of gold from Brazil which allowed the monarch to commission top architects, sculptors and artists, many from Italy. During the reign of the king's son, José I, an important school of sculpture was founded here.

Palácio Nacional de Mafra

Rising like a dark mirage across the plain stands the colossal **Palácio Nacional de Mafra** ❶ (Terreiro D.

Palácio Nacional de Mafra

João V, Mafra; www.palaciodemafra.pt; charge, basilica free), which is almost as large as Spain's El Escorial. Work began in 1717 and drew in a 50,000-strong army of labourers, artists and craftspeople to work on its thousand-odd rooms.

It was in the palace that the last king of Portugal, Manuel II, spent his final night before leaving for exile in October 1910, following the proclamation of the Republic. The grand abode was opened to the public the following year. Most of the finest furniture and paintings were taken to Brazil when João V fled from the French invasion in 1807, but an extensive collection of religious and historical works of art includes, in the Destinies Room, a graphic allegorical painting of the Duke of Wellington returning the nation to the king after its liberation from France.

Optional guided tours, which require reservations, last around ninety minutes and take you from the king's apartments at one end, through the splendid Baroque library, great domed basilica and plainer quarters, such as the pharmacy, long galleries and corridors, to the queen's apartments at the other – some 250m (800ft) away from the king's.

Basilica

The facade is a whopping 220m (720ft) long. The central point of the main facade is the **basilica** (free), flanked by two tall towers and built in Italian Baroque style. The bell towers boast the world's largest collection of bells, which can be heard for 24km (15 miles) when they are played on Sunday afternoons. The story goes that the king was informed that a single carillon of 49 bells would cost him 400,000.00 réis, an astronomical price for a country as small as Portugal. Offended by the suggestion, he replied 'So cheap? I'll take two!' Hence two carillons and 98 bells in all.

The basilica interior contains outstanding Portuguese and Italian sculpture, including fourteen large statues of saints in the vestibule, carved from Carrara marble. The church is unique in that it has six working organs, built at the same time and conceived to play together like an ensemble. Superb concerts are held here on the first Sunday of the month in summer.

Rococo library

Mafra's **library** is the undisputed highlight of the palace. One of the most important in Europe, it has a vaulted ceiling, precious wood floor and is full of Rococo splendour and light. The hugely wealthy João V sent ambassadors across Europe to bring back precious collections of books. There are well over 38,000 volumes, among them a sixteenth-century bible in five different languages, first editions of the great epic, *Os Lusíadas*

by Camões, and the earliest edition of *Homer* in Greek. Only researchers, historians and scholars are allowed access to the books, by appointment only. The library has been beautifully preserved, thanks in part to a colony of little bats behind the shelves who keep out paper-nibbling insects – they have been here since the sixteenth century.

The infirmary and state rooms

Beyond the simple monks' cells is the **infirmary**, the main room of the convent, a church with sixteen private sickrooms lining the nave so that patients could hear mass from their beds. Reserved for the most poorly of patients, the hospital had direct access to the cemetery. It is one of only four eighteenth-century infirmaries still in existence. It is followed by sumptuous state rooms, including the Throne Room, with frescoes and an ornate coffered ceiling, where official audiences with the king were held. In the South Tower, the Queen's Bedroom is of historic interest, for this is where the last king of Portugal, Manuel II, slept the night before sailing off into exile in Twickenham in 1910. A portrait of the monarch stands on an easel at the foot of the bed.

Mafra's spectacular library

For lunch you could choose from cafés or restaurants in Mafra, but Ericeira is a better bet with its choice of seafood.

Ericeira

The coastal resort and fishing village of **Ericeira** ❷ lies 10km (6 miles) northwest of Mafra. The quickest route by car is via the A21 but to avoid tolls you can take the slightly longer N116. Buses depart from just outside the palace.

With its 11km (7 miles) of beaches and first-class seafood restaurants, Ericeira sees an ever-increasing influx of Portuguese and foreign visitors, along with modern development on the outskirts. But fishing traditions carry on and at its heart is an enchanting old town. If you're travelling by car, head for the seafront and park in the Largo de San Sebastião. Walking along the waterfront southwards you'll come to the **Fishermen's Port**, where the day's catch is sold in the afternoon (no access for public). Keeping watch over the fishermen's beach is the **Capela de Santo António** (also known as the Chapel of our Lady of Safe Journeys). Every inch of this little chapel is tiled with blue and yellow *azulejos*. Outside, old-timers sit on tiled benches and watch the world go by. For centuries the bell and lantern which guided fishermen at night and in times of fog and storm were kept outside the church. A tiled panel here records, with some disdain, the historic event when Portugal's last king, Manuel II, hastily arrived from Mafra and boarded the royal yacht with his family from this little port to sail off into exile in the UK.

Mass at the Basilica of Mafra Palace

Old quarter

Sloping up from the seafront, the fishermen's village is a picturesque knot of cobbled, pedestrianised streets, sparkling white houses with blue-framed windows and doors, and tiled panelled scenes invoking divine protection against natural catastrophes.

For lunch options there are inviting *tascas*, *marisqueiras* (seafood specialists) or small bars with signs outside saying '*ha caracóis*' (we have snails). These tiny molluscs are cooked in broth and usually consumed with a chilled

The whitewashed streets of Ericeira

Food and drink

1 Mar à Vista
Rua de Santo António 16, Ericeira; www.mar-a-vista.eatbu.com; €€
Small and family-run, this authentic *marisqueira* has wonderful fresh shellfish. Come for *percebes* (goose barnacles), crab, clams, lobster or seafood cataplana. It's very popular, particularly with Portuguese, and it's worth booking a table.

2 Mar d'Areia
Rua da Fonte do Cabo 49, Ericeira; tel: 931-407 224; €€
Tucked away in a side street and full of locals, this place assures the freshest of fish, straight from the trawlers. It's simple and friendly, run by the same family for over seventy years. Pick your fish and see it sizzling on the grill before being served with a simple salad and boiled potatoes. Follow on with home-made dessert.

Sagres or Super Block beer. Above the **Praia dos Pescadores** (fishermen's beach) the family-run **Mar à Vista**, see 1, serves up great shellfish or try **Mar d'Areia**, see 2, near the fish market. After lunch walk a little way east for **Praça da República**, the lively main square with benches shaded by plane trees and surrounded by restaurants, cafés and shops.

Surfing the waves at Ericeira

Surfing mecca

Ericeira is Europe's first surfing reserve – only the second in the world. It has been known for its surfing community since the 1960s and championships have been held here since 1977. It is one of the rare places that brings together a variety of high-quality waves for all levels of surfer, at all times of the year. Several surf schools along the coast offer lessons and courses. The queen wave – and arguably the best in Portugal beyond Nazare's famed world-largest– is the long, fast and furious Coxos next to São Lourenço beach. Since attaining reserve status, this stretch of the coast and its flora and fauna are now protected.

The Carris Metropolitana bus will take you back to Lisbon. Driving via the A21 and A8 takes 45 minutes or more dependent on traffic.

Unspoilt, wild coast near Ericeira

TOUR 14
Queluz Palace

An easy half-day outing by train to a sumptuous pink palace and gardens with Versailles-style grandeur. The royal residence illustrates the evolution in Court tastes in the eighteenth and nineteenth century, from Baroque to Rococo and Neoclassicism.

DISTANCE: 14km (9 miles) by train from Lisbon, plus 1km (0.6 mile) on foot from the station
TIME: Leisurely half-day from Lisbon
START: Rossio Station, Lisbon
END: Queluz
POINTS TO NOTE: Queluz takes less than twenty minutes on the very frequent Sintra trains from Rossio Station; alight at Queluz-Belas. Exit the station on the left side, ie. where the train pulls in. Follow the signs to the palace (1km/0.6 mile, via Av. António Enes and Av. República). Tickets are available for the grounds only, or you can buy a combined ticket for the palace and grounds. For a meal at *Cozinha Velha*, book a table in advance.

Originally conceived as a summer retreat, Queluz became the royal family's favoured pleasure palace. They lived here from the mid-eighteenth century until their departure for Brazil in 1807, at the time of the French invasions. Queluz had its heyday during the reign of the sombre and devout Maria I (1777–99), but she suffered serious bouts of depression which deepened into severe mental health issues when her son José died of smallpox.

Pálacio Nacional de Queluz

The town is unprepossessing, and the palace facade is slightly shabby, but modesty is totally abandoned inside the **Palácio Nacional de Queluz** (Largo Palácio de Queluz; www.parquesdesintra.pt; charge). Though the palace lost much to French invasions (it was used by General Andoche Junot as his headquarters during the Peninsular War) and to a fire in 1934, it manages to preserve the air of eighteenth- to nineteenth-century royal privilege and luxury.

Palace interior

The lavish **Throne Room**, once the scene of balls and banquets, is adorned with colossal chandeliers, mirrors and gilt-layered walls and ceilings.

Queluz Palace

Beyond, the **Music Room** was the setting for operas, concerts and plays. Some of the concerts were performed here by the Queen's orchestra which, according to English traveller William Beckford, was the best in Europe. Summer gigs are still sometimes held here. The royal family's living rooms open out onto the immaculate Malta Gardens.

Next along is the **Corredor das Mangas** (Corridor of the Sleeves), with 1784 *azulejo* panels representing the continents and seasons as well as hunting scenes and depictions of everyday life. Continue to the **Sala dos Embaixadores** (Hall of Ambassadors), which has a floor like a chessboard, in addition to a wealth of mirrors and a *tromp l'oeil* ceiling showing the royal family attending a concert.

The final room is the **Don Quixote Chamber**, the royal bedroom, where Pedro IV, King of Portugal and first Emperor of Brazil, was born and died (1834). He was 9 years old when he fled Queluz with his family for Brazil during the Napoleonic invasion. A liberal-minded, charismatic and ambitious man, his life was always divided between Portugal and Brazil. He was perceived in Brazil as Portuguese, yet in Portugal was seen as a foreigner. He left numerous descendants both inside and outside of wedlock. The name of the room comes from the paintings based on Don Quixote's life.

Palace gardens

The palace gardens are the pride of Queluz, with clipped hedges in perfect geometric array, ponds, lakes and fountains, pavilions and armies of statues. The huge old magnolia trees

The ornate Throne Room

Statue in the palace gardens

and orange trees relieve some of the formality. The grounds were the setting for royal family parties, with guests entering via the pompous but original **Escadaria dos Leões** (Lions' Staircase). A stream, whose retaining walls are covered in *azulejos*, was diverted to pass through the palace grounds; the sluice gates closed so that the canal filled with water and the royal guests could view the tiled scenes from a boat. In the early nineteenth century, dozens of live animals – not just dogs, but lions and wolves – were boarded at Queluz, which was then the site of the royal zoo.

The palace and gardens make a spectacular setting from May until September for *Noites de Queluz* (Nights at Queluz), enchanting musical recreations from the eighteenth century on selected evenings.

Food and drink

1 Cozinha Velha

Palácio Nacional de Queluz, Largo Palácio; www.pousadas.pt; €€€
Within the former kitchens of the palace, this handsome restaurant retains – among other features – the old stone chimney and vaulted ceiling. Expect salt-cod dishes, clam cataplana, octopus or lobster salad and Chateaubriand. Be sure to leave space for the famous dessert buffet.

2 Retiro da Mina

Avenida da República 10, Queluz; tel: 214-352 978; €
Near the palace, this friendly, no-frills restaurant is popular with locals and offers great value. Come for grilled squid, salted cod, whole fresh fish or a barbecued half-chicken with chips and salad. Wash it down with incredibly cheap house wine – or choose a bottle from the wine list.

Eating in the palace

Separate from the main building are the ancient kitchens, now the setting of **Cozinha Velha**, see 1, the enticing restaurant run by the pousada opposite the palace. For something cheaper and more local, try **Retiro da Mina**, see 2, nearby, on the Avenida da República across the road from the palace.

Queluz's palace gardens

Escadaria dos Leões

DIRECTORY

Our edit of the best hotels, restaurants and evening entertainment to suit all tastes and budgets, plus an A–Z of all the essential information you need to know, a quick language guide, and some great book and film recommendations to give you a flavour of the city.

Accommodation

Lisbon's most appealing places to stay are found in the city centre, while the newer, more bland hotels (many with business facilities) are further out of town. Here, on the fringes, you get more bang for your buck, but you lack the sheer convenience of being near the centre, in a city of hills. The hotel scene has been burgeoning in recent years with a crop of new openings, many of them upmarket abodes and chic boutiques. Prices have been steadily creeping up, but Lisbon is still good value compared with most cities in Western Europe

In high season (June to September) rooms are at a premium, and you should book well ahead. Given the warm climate, spring and late autumn can be busy too, but in mid-winter prices can fall substantially. If you arrive on spec head for one of the tourist offices (see page 129), who will help you find accommodation.

Many hotels charge extra for breakfast; check when you make a reservation. Charges can be high (€17 per person for a four-star hotel, for instance) and many visitors prefer to head to the local café for coffee and pastries.

Be prepared for the city tourist tax, introduced in 2016, for those staying overnight in the capital. Since 2024, the charge has risen to €4 per adult, per night, subject to a maximum of seven nights, but not applicable to children under 14. The tax is not included on the rates advertised on booking websites and is charged directly to the guest on arrival.

Price categories

Each accommodation reviewed in this Guide is accompanied by a price category, based on the cost of a standard double room in high season. Prices include breakfast, service and VAT, unless stated otherwise, but exclude city tourist tax.

€€€€ = over €270
€€€ = €180–270
€€ = €100–180
€ = under €100

Alfama

Albergaria Senhora do Monte

Calçada do Monte 39; tram 28; www.hotelsenhoradomonte.com; €€

The steep climb up from the centre to this hotel, poised atop the highest of Lisbon's hills, is worth it for one of the finest views in the city. It has a panoramic bar and simple, spotless rooms, though these vary considerably in size; it's worth paying the extra for a balcony.

The fabulous terrace at *Memmo Alfama Design Hotel*

Memmo Alfama Design Hotel

Travessa das Merceeiras 27; tram 28; www.memmohotels.com; €€€

Expertly converted from a former bakery, the charming *Memmo Alfama* was the first boutique hotel in the Alfama. It is a stylish blend of old and new, and has a terrace with a small pool and bar offering spectacular river views.

Pousada Alfama

Rua de São Tomé 76; tram 28; www.pousadas.pt; €€€

Spread across a four-floor heritage building just back from Miradouro de São Vicente, *Pousada Alfama* offers some of Lisbon's finest Alfama and river views from its upper, terraced rooms. The decor is more contemporary and clean-lined than most other pousadas (which typically retain a greater number of original features), with street art by Portuguese artist Bordalo II and the chic *Manifesto Bar* adding modern flair.

Santiago de Alfama

Rua de Santiago 10–14; tram 28; www.santiagodealfama.com; €€€€

This palace turned intimate five-star boutique frames fine views of the Alfama and the Tagus from its upper floors. It has nineteen well-equipped rooms, a ground-floor café and a good restaurant serving modern Portuguese cuisine.

Solar do Castelo

Rua das Cozinhas 22; tram 28; www.solardocastelo.com; €€€€

This little gem, tucked within the walls of the castle, has just fourteen rooms and an inner courtyard and garden. It's so peaceful only the peacocks are likely to waken you. Breakfasts are generous. It's a steep climb from the centre – or an easy taxi ride.

Solar dos Mouros

Rua do Milagre de Santo António 6; bus #737 or tram 28; www.solardosmouroslisboa.com; €€€

A stylish boutique hotel up near the castle offering panoramic views over the Tagus and city. There are just thirteen rooms, each individually and creatively designed in contemporary style with striking modern paintings.

Baixa

Internacional Design Hotel

Rua da Betesga 3; metro: Rossio; www.idesignhotel.com; €€€

This cool designer hotel, in a great location overlooking Rossio, has four types of highly conceptualised, spectacular rooms: Urban, Tribe, Zen and Pop – with a magazine aesthetic and every comfort.

Nicola Rossio Hotel

Rua 1 de Dezembro 12; metro: Rossio; www.nicolarossiohotel.com; €€

Inspired by the neighbouring eighteenth-century *Café Nicola*, the hotel's 29 rooms (in standard or superior) are embellished with Art Deco flourishes. Some upper floors have views of Castelo de São Jorge.

The chic *Internacional Design Hotel*

Pestana CR7

Rua do Comércio 54; metro: Terreiro do Paço; www.pestanacr7.com; €€€€

A joint venture between Cristiano Ronaldo and the Pestana hotel group, this hip hotel in the city centre is a favourite of sports fans. There are plenty of screens for watching football or other sports, and walls are hung with shirts bearing Ronaldo's signature. Multifunctional designer guest rooms have huge smart TVs with Apple TV and Android streaming.

Pestana Pousada Lisboa

Praça do Comércio 31–34; metro: Terreiro do Paço; www.pousadas.pt; €€€

Lisbon's main pousada has a prime location, comfortable classic rooms and attentive service. It also has an excellent restaurant, and diners can sit beneath the vaults or outside with fine views of the square.

Turim Terreiro do Paço Hotel

Rua do Comércio 9; metro: Terreiro do Paço; www.turim-hotels.com; €€

This hotel has a handy location just north of the main Praça do Comércio. Staff are really friendly, rooms are modern and soundproofed but devoid of storage for clothes and luggage.

Avenida da Liberdade/ North Lisbon

Avenida Palace

Rua 1 de Dezembro 123; metro: Rossio; www.hotelavenidapalace.pt; €€€€

Situated on Rossio, the remodelled *Avenida Palace* is one of Lisbon's finest luxury hotels. Built in 1892 it has a magnificent, old-fashioned elegance, with sumptuous public rooms and beautiful classically decorated guestrooms. Sybarites can opt for the Louis XVI-style room.

Britania

Rua Rodrigues Sampaio 17; metro: Avenida; www.lisbonheritagehotels.com; €€

One of Lisbon's most charming and intimate hotels, this 1940s townhouse alongside the main Avenida da Liberdade has been lovingly restored with genuine Art Deco touches. The rooms are spacious and elegantly appointed, with marble bathrooms.

Corinthia Hotel Lisbon

Avenida Columbano Bordalo Pinheiro 105; metro: Jardim Zoológico; www.corinthia.com; €€€

This five-star hotel is a peaceful and stylish sanctuary after a busy day of sightseeing. Luxe decor, live music in the *Tempus Bar*, a sumptuous ESPA spa and second-to-none service make the *Corinthia* stand out from the rest. There's an indoor swimming pool and gym, *Erva Restaurant* for Portuguese specialities, and the glamorous *Soul Bar* for cocktails.

Dom Pedro Palace

Avenida Engenheiro Duarte Pacheco 24; metro: Marquês de Pombal; www.dompedro.com; €€€

An upmarket room at the *Four Seasons Hotel Ritz Lisbon*

The swish five-star *Dom Pedro Palace* has 23 floors of guestrooms and spectacular views of the city. Popular with American tourists and European business travellers, it has a top-flight Italian restaurant, a bistro-style café, indoor pool, a spa and fitness centre, and is a stone's throw from the famous Amoreiras Shopping Centre.

Epic Sana Lisboa Hotel

Avenida Engenheiro Duarte Pacheco 15; metro: Marquês de Pombal or Parque; www.sanahotels.com; €€€

Five-star contemporary abode with infinity rooftop pool and large spa and fitness centre. It's slightly out of the centre in Amoreiras, but you can walk to the metro in just over ten minutes or take a taxi to the centre.

Eurostars Das Letras

Rua Castilho 6–12; metro: Avenida; www.eurostardasletras.com; €€€

Part of a Spanish chain, this is a good-value, contemporary hotel. The theme is literature, with shelves of books and each room dedicated to an acclaimed author – Virgil, Shakespeare, Cervantes, Stendhal. An extract from the writer's work, in its original language, can be found above the bedhead.

Expo Astória

Rua Braamcamp 10; metro: Marquês de Pombal; www.hotelexpoastoria.com-hotel.com; €

This attractive Art Deco hotel has spacious rooms and is just a short hop

Room at the *Pestana CR7*

from Praça de Marquês de Pombal, with its metro station. Staff are courteous, breakfasts decent and, given the location, it ranks as a bargain.

Florida Hotel

Rua Duque de Palmela 34; metro: Marquês de Pombal; www.hotel-florida.pt; €€

The *Florida* is a quirky haunt with decor inspired by 1950s and 1960s movies, and a restaurant called *The Great American Disaster*. Some rooms are small and it's a little north of the centre, but prices are good for a four-star, breakfasts are above-average and staff friendly.

Four Seasons Hotel Ritz Lisbon

Rua Rodrigues da Fonseca 88; metro: Marquês de Pombal; www.fourseasons.com; €€€€

The *Four Seasons Hotel Ritz Lisbon*'s pool

The utilitarian 1950s building belies a swanky hotel that is the height of indulgence. The 282 deluxe rooms all have marble bathrooms, views over the green Parque Edward VII and, if you're lucky, a private terrace. The hotel boasts a gastronomic restaurant, sushi lounge, state-of-the-art spa and Sodashi treatment menu.

Inspira Liberdade Boutique Hotel

Rua de Santa Marta 48; metro: Avenida or Marquês do Pombal; www.inspirahotels.com; €€€

Near the Avenida da Liberdade, this designer bolthole has admirable eco-credentials – it uses green technology, runs according to sustainable policies and supports charitable projects. Rooms and spa are modelled around feng shui principles.

Lisboa Plaza

Travessa do Salitre 7; metro: Avenida; www.lisbonplazahotel.com; €€€

Off Avenida Liberdade, on a quiet street, the charming *Lisboa Plaza* opened in the 1950s and has been in the hands of the same family ever since. It has comfortable traditional rooms and very accommodating staff. Generous breakfasts, too.

Porto Bay Liberdade

Rua Rosa Araújo 8; metro: Marquês de Pombal; www.portobay.com; €€€

A five-star hotel converted from three early-twentieth-century palaces. Behind its perfectly preserved historic facade, the interiors are modern and chic; each of the 98 rooms come complete with USB chargers, large smart TVs and pillow menu. There's an indoor pool, gym and spa.

Tivoli Avenida Liberdade

Avenida da Liberdade 185; metro: Avenida; www.tivolihotels.com; €€€

One of Lisbon's largest and longest-running luxury hotels, the *Tivoli* is right on the main thoroughfare, close to top designer stores. One of Lisbon's hottest night spots, it features a cool new Art Deco rooftop restaurant, sky bar and nightly DJs.

Valverde

Avenida da Liberdade 164; metro: Avenida; www.valverdehotel.com; €€€

Ideally situated for shopaholics on the elegant Avenida da Liberdade, this charming hotel has antique prints and art, fine fabrics and retro furnishings. The ground-floor *Sítio* restaurant, with excellent Portuguese cuisine, overlooks the courtyard. Staff are delightful, and there's a heated pool and fitness centre.

VIP Executive Éden

Praça dos Restauradores 24; metro: Restauradores; www.viphotels.com; €€€

A famous Art Deco cinema reimagined as a cool, modern apartment-hotel. Excellent value, especially for families. There are kitchen-equipped studios, full apartments, a panoramic pool, a terrace bar and breakfast service.

Chic style at the *Bairro Alto Hotel*

Bairro Alto/Chiado/ Príncipe Reale

Bairro Alto Hotel

Praça Luís de Camões 2; tram 28; www.bairroaltohotel.com; €€€€

Ultra-chic five-star boutique in the Bairro Alto, with 55 rooms spanning six different categories, an excellent restaurant and the top-floor *BA Terrace* overlooking the river and rooftops – a great spot for lunch, afternoon cocktails or a candlelit drink.

Hotel Borges Chiado

Rua Garrett 108; metro: Baixa-Chiado; www.hotelborges.com; €€

This typical old Lisbon bolthole has plenty of character and a great location, right by the metro and close to the restaurants and elegant shops of the Chiado. The best rooms have balconies. Ask for one on a higher floor to avoid street noise.

Hotel do Chiado

Rua Nova do Almada 114; metro: Baixa-Chiado; www.hoteldochiadolisbon.com; €€€

This four-star has a perfect location in the heart of Lisbon, with excellent shopping and a great choice of eateries nearby, plus one of the best rooftops in the city. Rooms are furnished in a contemporary style; the pick of the bunch have a terrace and view.

LX Boutique Hotel

Rua Do Alecrim 12; metro: Cais do Sodré; www.lxboutiquehotel.com; €€

Fashionable boutique hotel with chic rooms and arty themes. Guestrooms come with all modern amenities – the best overlook the river across the rooftops. The bar-lounge becomes a sushi, salad and tapas restaurant between 12.30pm and 2pm; every afternoon, complimentary sushi is served.

Memmo Príncipe Real

Rua Dom Pedro V 56; metro: Rato; www.memmohotels.com; €€€€

In the bohemian enclave of Príncipe Real, this five-star gem has stunning contemporary interior design, a rooftop pool with panoramic city views and (on the same level) a restaurant for breakfast, light lunches, cocktails and dinner.

Lapa

As Janelas Verdes

Rua das Janelas Verdes 47; tram 15; www.asjanelasverdes.com; €€€

Next to the National Museum of Ancient Art, with views of the Tagus, this romantic little hotel occupies the eighteenth-century townhouse of one of Portugal's most famous writers, Eça de Queirós. In summer, breakfast is taken in the quiet, garden-like courtyard.

Olissippo Lapa Palace

Rua do Pau de Bandeira 4; tram 25 or bus #727; www.olissippohotels.com; €€€€

This beautifully converted palatial mansion overlooks the River Tagus in the classy Lapa neighbourhood. Opened in 1992, it remains one of the

Porto Bay Liberdade suite with balcony

city's most sumptuous and expensive hotels. It is surrounded by landscaped gardens and has an outdoor pool.

York House

Rua das Janelas Verdes 32; tram: 25 or bus 727; www.yorkhouselisboa.com; €€

Converted from a seventeenth-century Carmelite convent, this small hotel retains the feel of a serene retreat. It was opened as a guesthouse in 1880 by a couple of Yorkshire women (hence the name) and its English guests have included authors Graham Greene and John le Carré. Meals in summer are served in the plant-filled courtyard.

Belém

Altis Belém Hotel & Spa

Doca do Bom Sucesso; tram 15E; www.altishotels.com; €€€€

Part of the Altis chain, this award-winning five-star design hotel has wonderful views over the River Tagus in Belém. Enjoy gourmet cuisine in the *Feitoria* restaurant (see page 66), riverside cocktails, a state-of-the-art spa and contemporary guestrooms.

Jerónimos 8

Rua dos Jerónimos 8; tram 15E; www.almeidahotels.pt; €€€

Go boutique in Belém at this stylish place, with sleek rooms that combine strong and neutral colours to harmonious effect. There are great views over the monastery. The hip red-and-white *Bussaco Wine Bar* serves rare Portuguese bottles, simple dishes and delicious *pastéis de Belém* (custard tarts).

Parque das Nações

Myriad by Sana

Cais das Naus, Lote 2.21.01; metro: Moscavide or Oriente; www.myriad.pt; €€€€

At the northern end of the park and linked to the Vasco da Gama Tower, this sophisticated hotel is all light and water. It stands right on the wide estuary of the Tagus – so wide it looks like the sea – and makes the most of the views of the river and the Ponte Vasco da Gama. Decor is contemporary and stylish throughout. The 176 guest rooms come with Nespresso coffee machines, bathrobes and the option of a whirlpool bath or shower with massage jets.

Sintra

Penha Longa Resort

Estrada da Lagoa Azul; www.ritzcarlton.com; €€€€

Flanked by mountain greenery, this salmon-hued fourteenth-century monastery has been transformed into one of Sintra's most luxurious and secluded stays. On site, there are two Michelin-recognised restaurants, an indulgent spa and an 18-hole championship golf course. It's a true bolthole away from the palace's crowds.

São Miguel Guest House

Rua Soto Maior 15; tel: 219-244 088; €€

A gem of a guesthouse just down the road from the centre of Sintra. Teresa is a wonderfully welcoming host and, like owner Mafalda, a font of knowledge on

The cosy library at *As Janelas Verdes*

Sintra and beyond. Dating mainly from the nineteenth century, the house has period furnishings, elegant rooms and romantic views over the hills of Sintra. Breakfast is a treat, everything fresh and delicious, and weather permitting, is taken in the garden amid jacarandas, wisteria and roses.

Cascais, Estoril and Queluz

Hotel Palácio Estoril

Rua Particular, Estoril; www.palacioestorilhotel.com; €€€€

This 1930-opened five-star hotel is as palatial as the name suggests and during World War II, due to Portugal's neutrality, it became the favoured haunt of European royalty, as well as British and German spies. Today, it offers modern comfort and amenities but retains the charm from a bygone era. Guests are entitled to special rates at its famous golf course.

The Pergola Boutique

Avenida Valbom 13, Cascais; www.thepergola.pt; €€€

A nineteenth-century manor house with ten individually furnished rooms. An excellent breakfast is served in the flower-filled garden, or by the fireplace in winter; complimentary port is served daily every afternoon; massage treatments can be arranged in your room on request. Anything else, just ask the staff, who are wonderfully helpful and friendly.

Pousada Palácio de Queluz

D. Maria I, Largo do Palácio Nacional, Queluz; www.pousadas.pt; €€€

Altis Belém Hotel & Spa

A Baroque-style building with a five-stage bell tower, this was part of the summer palace that was formerly the domain of the Royal Guard of the Court. The pousada has elegant, well-sized rooms in traditional style.

Arrábida Peninsula

Palmela

Pousada do Castelo de Palmela

Castelo de Palmela; www.pousadas.pt; €€€

A hilltop hotel in a converted monastery with wonderful views of the Serra da Arrábida. It forms part of a medieval castle which was snatched from the Moors by King Afonso Henriques in the twelfth century. Sink into a large comfy chair in the cloisters and dine on fine Portuguese fare in the former refectory.

Hotel Palácio Estoril has a storied history

Restaurants

Culinary hotspots have been springing up all over the city in recent years and there is now a huge diversity in the dining scene. An *ementa turística* is a fixed (not tourist) menu offered by many restaurants, particularly at lunchtime. It can be excellent value, typically including bread, soup, main course and dessert with a glass of wine, beer or soft drink. Also worth trying is the *prato do dia* or dish of the day. When ordering wine you can't go too far wrong ordering the house *(vinho da casa)*; ask the waiter for *tinto* (red), *branco* (white) or *vinho verde* (green wine).

Opening times are lunch *(almoço)*, from noon until 3pm, and dinner *(jantar)*, from 7.30pm to at least 10pm, often much later. Locals tend to dine after 9pm so if you want the buzz, leave eating until later. Most restaurants close between lunch and dinner sittings but there are dozens of cafés and teashops open all day for sandwiches or savoury and sweet pastries.

Alfama/Santa Apolónia

A Parreirinha do Paraíso

Rua do Paraíso 40C; metro: Santa Apolónia; www.instagram.com/aparreirinhadoparaiso; €

Simple, traditional dishes at fair prices makes *A Parreirinha do Paraíso* worth the slight detour from Alfama proper. Come for *bitoque* (steak topped with egg), codfish cakes or whole grilled sea bream, and enjoy the atmosphere of the still fairly local crowd.

Price categories

Each restaurant and café reviewed in this Guide is accompanied by a price category, based on the cost of a two-course meal (or similar) for one, including a glass of house wine.

€€€€ = over €60

€€€ = €35–60

€€ = €20–35

€ = up to €20

Sardinha

Rua do Jardim do Tabaco 18; bus #734; tel: 218-867 437; €€

As typical as you can get, this pocket-sized restaurant on the edge of Alfama is wonderfully unfussy, with simple, seasonal sardines being the speciality. House wine, served in terracotta jugs, is a steal, as are the hearty soups. This is humble, homely dining at its best.

Baixa/Cais do Sodré

O Castico

Rua dos Sapateiros 81; bus #711 or #736; tel: 213-472 070; €€

One of the more authentic and less touristy-priced restaurants in Baixa,

The unmissable Time Out Mercado da Riberia

this wooden-panelled dining room is a reliable spot to enjoy seafood rice, grilled octopus, clams perfectly steamed in wine or *bacalhau com natas* (creamed codfish) at fair prices.

Pap'Açorda

Mercado da Ribeira, Avenida 24 de Julho; metro: Cais do Sodré; www.papacorda.com; €€

Thirty-five years in the heart of the Bairro Alto, *Pap'Açorda* moved to modern premises on the first floor of the Time Out Mercado da Ribeira, but the Portuguese classic fare is every bit as good as it was. Try the signature dish – the fabulous and filling *açorda real* (thick shellfish stew with lobster and shrimp), followed by the famous chocolate mousse.

Time Out Mercado da Ribeira

Avenida 24 de Julho 50; metro: Cais do Sodré; www.timeoutmarket.com; €€

Occupying half of the old Mercado da Ribeira, Lisbon's market hall, this uber-cool Time Out food market combines an affordable gourmet experience with a practical approach and a laid-back atmosphere. Since it opened in 2014, Lisboetas and tourists have been flocking here for both snacks and full meals from over forty outlets. Go at any time of the day, select from the specialities of Portugal's leading chefs, grab a glass of wine or fizz from a top supplier, find a space at one of the long wooden tables and enjoy.

Bairro Alto/Chiado/Príncipe Real

100 Maneiras

Rua do Teixeira 39; bus #202 or #758, Elevador da Glória; www.100maneiras.com; €€€€

This intimate, elegant restaurant in Bairro Alto is foodie heaven, offering a tasting menu from €140 where each dish is a surprise. Serbian chef Ljubomir Stanisic also has a more informal, cheaper bistro at 9 Largo Trindade in Chiado.

A Cevicheria

Rua Dom Pedro V 129; metro: Restauradores; www.acevicheria.pt; €€€

Since opening, this tiny Peruvian restaurant has made waves on the culinary scene. You can't book in advance, but at least while you wait (and it may be for 1–2hr), you can knock back a pisco sour and Peruvian popcorn at a pavement table. Expect fabulous flavours and combinations, beautifully presented dishes and a buzzing ambience. The ceviche is divine. The dominant decor is a giant octopus on the ceiling, crafted in sponge.

Alma

Rua Anchieta 15; metro: Baixa-Chiado; www.almalisboa.pt; €€€€

Celebrity chef Henrique Sá Pessoa is well known for innovative Portuguese cuisine with a touch of the East. For a variety of his exquisite creations at this two-Michelin-starred restaurant, splash out on the wallet-squeezing Alma menu (€190 per person), paired with the best of national wines.

By the Wine

Rua das Flores 41–43, Chiado; tram 28 or bus #202 or #758; www.bythewine.pt; €€

This is the flagship store of José Maria da Fonseca. Wines are served with a range of local delicacies such as ibérico ham, Azeitão cheese, salmon ceviche and oysters from the Sado Estuary.

Cantinho do Avillez

Rua dos Duques de Bragança 7; tram 28 or metro: Baixa-Chiado; www.cantinhodoavillez.pt; €€€

The sister restaurant of José Avillez's two-Michelin-starred *Belcanto* nearby (see page 48), offering the famous chef's dishes at more affordable prices. The ambience is informal and relaxed, with retro decor and friendly, professional service. Among Avillez's celebrated dishes are deep-fried green beans with tartar sauce, cod with breadcrumbs, egg and 'exploding' olives, and giant red shrimps with Thai flavours.

Cervejaria da Trindade

Rua Nova da Trindade 20; bus #202 or #758, tram 28; www.cervejariatrindade.pt; €€

This famous old beer hall and restaurant within a former monastery has spectacular panels of *azulejos* decorating the walls and serves popular Portuguese dishes and seafood specialities. Caters for large groups and has a hundred seats outside.

Minibar

Rua António Maria Cardoso 58; metro: Baixa-Chiado; www.minibar.pt; €€€€

This was famous chef José Avillez's first gourmet bar. Within the São Luiz Theatre, the evening-only venue is all about small gastronomical delicacies and finger food, created to surprise and entertain. A 'Ferrero Rocher chocolate', for example, will turn out to be foie gras.

Sea Me

Rua do Loreto 21; metro: Baixa-Chiado, tram 28; www.peixariamoderna.com; €€€

Choose from a fish market-like display of fresh seafood – or a lobster or crab from the tanks. There are sushi and sashimi options, salmon ceviche, seared tuna with wasabi ice cream, turbot, mullet, sole – and plenty more. Reservations recommended.

Taberna da Rua das Flores

Rua das Flores 103; tram 28 or metro: Baixa-Chiado; www.taberneiros.pt; €€

Don't let the queues put you off this tiny, old-fashioned *taberna*. You can't reserve in advance, but you can either arrive early (preferably before 7pm) or come later and queue with a drink or give your name and return later. Tapas include seafood, ceviche, goat's cheese and historic Lisbon dishes such as *iscas* (pork liver), sweetbreads or *mexilhões à bulhão pato* (mussels with coriander, garlic and lemon). Leave room for the Portuguese almond cake, *toucinho do céu*, 'bacon from heaven', so-called because the recipe includes pork lard.

Tágide Wine & Tapas

Largo da Academia Nacional de Belas Artes 18; metro: Baixa-Chiado or tram 28; www.restaurantetagide.com; €

Cervejaria da Trindade is a well-known beer hall

Enjoy excellent tapas, Portuguese wines and great city views in this elegant bar below the well-known *Tágide Restaurant*. Typical tapas here include fried quail's egg and game chips, Iberian ham or clams with white wine and garlic. There's often live jazz or DJs on weekend evenings.

Avenida and North Lisbon

Bon Jardim

Travessa Santo Antão 11; metro: Restauradores; tel: 213-424 389; €

A good budget option, this simple place serves large helpings of chicken piri-piri (with chilli sauce) along with fries and a simple salad. Speedy service.

Cervejaria Ramiro

Avenida Almirante Reis 1; metro: Intendente; www.cervejariaramiro.pt; €€€€

Long-established, family-run beer house that offers some of the best fresh seafood in the city. It's all laid out for you: huge red shrimps, goose barnacles (*percebes*), grilled giant tiger prawns, oysters, clams and crab. If you still have

Pavement dining in Bairro Alto

room, follow on with a *prego* (steak sandwich). No reservations so expect queues, but slick service once you're in.

Os Tibetanos

Rua do Salitre 117; metro: Avenida; www.ostibetanos.com; €

This was the first vegetarian restaurant to open in Lisbon. It offers Tibetan pastries, seitan 'steak' in mushroom sauce and crêpes with tofu. For desserts, try the rose-petal ice cream or the wickedly decadent dolma tart, combining chestnuts and chocolate.

O Talho

Rua Carlos Testa 1B; metro: São Sebastião; www.otalho.com; €€€€

A carnivore's delight, combining a butcher's shop and restaurant. Award-winning chef Kiko looks for new ways to cook and taste meat in his 'laboratory kitchen'. One of the favourite dishes is beef tartare, prepared at the table.

Vegetariano PSI

Alameda Santo António Capuchos; metro: Avenida; tel: 213-590 573; €

Expect a riot of exquisite flavours and colours at this excellent vegetarian restaurant. Among the menu offerings are mango ceviche, beetroot humous, veggie curries and seitan kebabs. Attractive garden setting. No alcohol.

Estrela and south

Café de São Bento

Rua de São Bento 212; tram 28; www.cafesaobento.com; €€€

Next to the Palácio da Assembléia da República, home to Portugal's parliament, this restaurant opened in 1982 with the aim of recreating the Lisbon cafés of old, serving traditional *bife á marrare* (steak in a creamy pepper sauce). Its steaks have won many awards. Follow on with divine *tarte tatin*, served with ice cream.

Mercado de Campo de Ourique

Rua Coelho da Rocha; tram 28; www.instagram.com/mercadodecampodeourique; €€

The 1930s marketplace has been given a revamp and is now a fresh and lively rendezvous for the city. Fruit, fish and veg stalls are joined by an array of food outlets where you can choose from take-away sushi and seafood, *petiscos* (small sharing plates), gourmet burgers or steak and chips, and sit at informal tables in the food hall.

Solar dos Nunes

Rua dos Lusíadas 68, Alcântara; bus #724 or tram 15; www.solardosnunes.com; €€€

A delightful rustic restaurant specialising in Alentejo dishes such as *ameijoas à alentejano* (clam and pork casserole) and black pork loin with bread and garlic. Seafood soup is a good bet, or you can select fish from the tank. A fixed-price lunch menu offers excellent value, alongside a great wine list.

Belém

À Margem

Doca Jardim do Bom Sucesso; tram 15; tel: 918-620 032; €€

Restaurants and bars in the former docks

Trendy café in a converted shipping container by the riverside. Come for snacks, salads – or just a glass of wine while you watch the boats go by.

Guelra

Rua de Belém 35; tram 15; www.guelraott.com; €€€

Seafood is the main link between the pair of similar but distinct dining concepts across *Guelra*'s two levels. Head to the *First Floor* restaurant at lunch to enjoy the excellent-value three-course, all-fish testing menu, or come in the evening for the seven-course option paired with wines.

O Pedrouços

Doca de Belém; tram 15; tel: 962-381 795; €€

Right on the Tejo, this has great river views from the outdoor tables or, inside, through the picture windows. It is popular with locals and tourists alike, offering friendly service, delicious shellfish risotto and fabulously fresh, simply cooked sea bass and turbot. Good value.

Po Tat

Rua Bartolomeu Dias 117; tram 15; www.potatrestaurant.com; €€€

Set in the impressive Palácio do Governador in Belém, *Po Tat* – the name of the famous Portuguese egg tarts in Cantonese – fuses local flavours with culinary influences from Portugal's former Asian colonies and neighbouring nations. All plates are perfectly stylised, but the fragrant flavours of kimchi, miso and curried sauces steal the show.

Po Tat

Cascais

Fortaleza do Guincho

Estrada do Guincho; bus #405 and #415 from Cascais; www.fortalezadoguincho.pt; €€€€

Expect the highest-quality fish and seafood from Portuguese waters, paired with outstanding wines and wonderful views of the Atlantic and Cabo da Roca. It's also a five-star hotel and member of the Relais et Chateaux group.

Sult

Rua das Flores 10A; www.sultcascais.pt; €€€€

In Danish, *sult* means 'hunger' – and hungry is how you should arrive. Chef Nelson Soares's fusion menu is phenomenal, blending Italian and local flavours in genius ways, such as Iberian black pork ragù and arancini stuffed with Azeitão cheese. The dimly lit, cosy dining room adorned with black-and-white retro photographs adds to the appeal.

Fortaleza do Guincho

Nightlife

Lisbon's nightlife is as diverse as you would expect of a modern European capital city. You'll find trendy bars, late-night clubs, *fado* houses, atmospheric *tabernas* and music to suit all tastes. For events and listings pick up the monthly Portuguese/English booklet, *Follow Me Lisboa*, free from tourist offices and some hotels. Remember to take cash with you – many venues don't accept credit cards. See also Entertainment on page 22 for information on the performing arts.

Rooftop bars

Park

Calçada do Combro 58; tram 28; www.facebook.com/parklisboaofficial

A popular chillout spot on the roof of a Bairro Alto multistorey car park surrounded by greenery, with jazz, funk and soul music and wonderful views of the Tagus. Also well known for its daily cultural and musical programme.

Silk

Rua da Misericórdia 14; metro: Baixa-Chiado or tram 28; www.silk-club.com

Luxurious and sophisticated private club (and sushi restaurant) six floors up, with a summer terrace and great views of the Lisbon skyline.

SEEN Sky Bar

Hotel Tivoli Lisboa, Avenida da Liberdade 185; metro: Avenida; www.seenlx.com

Kick back on comfy sofas at this stylish bar on the top floor of the *Hotel Tivoli Lisboa* and enjoy music, fine dining and a dazzling vista of the city.

Topo

Centro Comercial, Praça Martim Moniz; metro: Martim Moniz; www.topo-lisboa.pt

This trendy spot atop a shopping centre blends arcade games and international food with late-night DJs, decent cocktails and views across the city towards Castelo de São Jorge.

Nightclubs

Pensão Amor

Rua do Alecrim 19, Cais do Sodré; metro: Cais do Sodré; www.pensaoamor.pt

A former brothel in an erstwhile red-light quarter, this lively club offers burlesque cabaret performances, jazz concerts, pole-dancing exhibitions, DJ soirées – and great cocktails. Decadent, fun decor more than hints at the history of the venue: deep red velvet furnishings, vintage mirrors, sensual paintings and saucy posters. Rooms of all shapes and sizes extend across three floors.

Harbour

Cais do Gás, Armazém A Porta 7; metro: Cais do Sodré; www.harbourmusic.pt

With river views, thumping electronic music, and afterparties that often continue beyond sunrise, weekend-only *Harbour* has one of the best atmospheres of any late-

Tipples at the Time Out Mercado da Riberia

night Lisbon venue. Payments are made via a card issued on arrival; keep track of your consumption and don't lose the card.

Trumps

Rua da Imprensa Nacional 104; tram 24E; www.trumps.pt

One of Lisbon's most popular LGBTQ+ venues, *Trumps* promises a fabulous night out to all – though it can get uncomfortably crowded. Nights usually start with drag performances before DJs keep the party going into the early hours.

Bars

Chapitô

Costa do Castelo 7; bus #73; www.chapito.org

Take in jaw-dropping city views over a sundowner at this bar near the castle. Tapas and hearty Portuguese fare are also on offer. *Chapitô* is a non-profit organisation offering training through performing arts, and the complex includes a theatre and circus school. Salsa nights are sometimes held in the basement.

Cinco Lounge

Rua Ruben António Leitão 17A; metro: Rato or bus #773; www.cincolounge.com

Seductive and sophisticated British-owned bar with great cocktails, made of fresh fruit and spices, with and without alcohol. Unusually, the music has decibel levels that enable conversation.

Casas de fado

Prices for food are noticeably higher than restaurants (around €50 per person) but that of course includes the *fado* show. There is often a minimum charge until 10/11pm, typically €30/35, which goes towards your meal, then later it's €10–20. See also *Parreirinha de Alfama* and *O Faia*, Walk 3.

Café Luso

Travessa da Queimada 10; tram 28 or bus #758; www.cafeluso.pt

The atmospheric *Café Luso* has hosted *fado* and folk dances since 1827, making it the oldest *fado* house in Bairro Alto. Artists sing from 10pm until 2am and food is available.

Maria da Mouraria

Largo da Severa; metro:Martim Moniz; www.mariadamouraria.eatbu.com

Mouraria is said to be the birthplace of *fado*, and this atmospheric restaurant is still one of Lisbon's best dining places during a performance. In summer, tables and singers spill out onto the square in front.

Casinos

Casino Estoril

Avenida Dr Stanley Ho, Estoril; trains from Cais do Sodré; www.casino-estoril.pt

The second-largest casino in Europe, this is a big draw for gamblers and was the inspiration for Ian Fleming's *Casino Royale*. Passports are required. There is also a choice of restaurants, including the excellent *Mandarim*. Since 2006 the casino has seen competition from the Casino Lisboa at the Parque das Nações (www.casino-lisboa.pt).

Essentials

Accessible travel

Lisbon's cobbled streets and steep hills don't make it easy for disabled travellers and although accessible facilities have greatly improved, it is not an ideal destination for disabled people. Areas such as Belém, parts of Baixa and Parque das Nações (the most accessible of all) are easier to navigate, as they are flat with broad streets and pavements. Several metro stations lack full accessible facilities. Vintage trams are overcrowded and unsuitable for wheelchairs, and many of the modern tram stops have steps. Carris (www.carris.pt) offers a bus service for those with reduced mobility, for which you will need to book ahead. Some buses have access ramps and spaces for wheelchairs. Taxis are often the best option – especially to the castle. Drivers tend to be helpful and friendly, and prices are low.

Budgeting

Accommodation

A double room in a simple hotel costs €40–100, in the mid-range category €100–150 and for a four-star plus, expect to pay over €200. Most prices do not include breakfast. Rates fluctuate according to the season and are usually at their highest from May to September and lowest in January and February.

Drinks and meals

A coffee costs anything from €0.90 (espresso in a local bar) to €3 (cappuccino served in a smart bar on a main square); beer is €1.50–3. Most restaurants offer a midday meal bargain, called an *ementa* turística, often no more than 15 for a fixed-price, three-course meal. Come evening, a three-course meal with wine in a mid-range restaurant would be around €30, or in an upmarket restaurant from €50 upwards.

Museums

Admission fees range from €2.50 up to €20. A few museums have a free day or half-day; for instance, the Calouste Gulbenkian is free on a Sunday after 2pm, though some free sessions are now solely for residents, rather than visitors. There are normally fifty percent discounts for students, young persons, families over four persons and visitors aged 65 and over. Children up to 12 are usually free.

Transport

A taxi from the airport to the city centre costs around €18; rideshares are usually cheaper and the metro

Tiled scene of a pre-earthquake Praça do Comércio

even more so. A single ticket costs €2.10 on buses, €1.85 on the metro, €3.10 on trams, and is reduced to €1.50 if using a pre-paid card (€0.50), which can be purchased from metro stations and ticket machines. You can charge it for a 24hr session, which costs €7 and is valid for unlimited journeys on the Carris network (the latter includes metro, buses, trams and funiculars such as the Elevador de Sant Justa). If you're travelling around the city for more than a day, consider a reloadable Viva Viagem card – though the acceptance of contactless bankcards on the Carris network since 2024 have made these cards less necessary for visitors. Lisbon's tourist offices offer a discount Lisboa Card that entitles holders to free metro, bus, tram and lift transport, entry into 51 museums and monuments, and discounts on tourist attractions such as city tours and certain shops. The card is available for 24hr, 48hr or 72hr at €27, €44 and €54, respectively, with substantial reductions for children.

Children

With its vintage trams, funiculars, elevators and ferries and river trips, Lisbon offers some great ways to entertain children just by touring around the city. Catch the cheap ferry to Cacilhas across the river and take bus #101 to the Cristo Rei statue, where a lift whisks visitors up to a cool viewing platform. Alternatively, you could board a bus from Cacilhas to explore the beaches of Costa da Caparica.

The indisputable number one Lisbon attraction for children is the Oceanarium at the Parque das Nações (see page 68), which is one of the biggest in the world. The park also has playgrounds, fountains, aerial cable cars and a hands-on science museum. The Jardim Zoológico (Zoo, Estrada be Benfica 158–160; metro: Jardim Zoológico; www.zoo.pt) has two thousand animals, plus a cable car and miniature train. Shows feeding of pelicans and sea lions. The Museu da Marioneta (Puppet Museum, see page 57) has puppets from all over the world and stages shows. For children the most entertaining of the city tours is the amphibious HIPPOtrip (www.hippotrip.com), which tours the centre, then plunges into the river.

Children under 4 years travel free of charge on public transport; those between 4 and 12 pay half-price.

Clothing

Take comfy walking shoes for the steep hills and uneven cobbled streets. Spring and autumn are relatively balmy, so you won't need anything heavier than a sweater in the daytime and light jacket at night. Summer days can be very hot but pack a wrap

Postcards from Lisbon

or jumper for cooler, windy evenings. Winters are mild but you will need warmer clothes and rainwear.

Crime and safety

Lisbon traditionally has been one of Europe's more laid-back and safe capitals, but as with any major city, pickpocketing can be an issue. Leave valuables in the hotel safe and keep an eye on handbags, mobile phones and wallets. Be particularly alert on public transport (especially Tram 28), in cafés on Rossio, the Alfama, markets and other tourist hotspots. Report theft to the nearest police station or local tourist office. The police emergency number is 112. At night, take care around the narrow dark streets of the Mouraria, Alfama and Graça. Always lock cars and never leave anything of value in view.

Customs

Free exchange of non-duty-free goods for personal use is allowed between countries within the EU. Those from non-EU countries should refer to their home country's regulating organisation for a current list of import restrictions. Non-EU residents may be able to reclaim VAT on some items bought within Portugal.

Electricity

The electrical current in Portugal is 220V; AC and sockets take two-pin, round-pronged plugs. For US appliances, 220v transformers and plug adaptors are required.

Embassies

Australia (Embassy) Avenida da Liberdade 200; tel: 213-101 500; www.portugal.embassy.gov.au.
Canada (Embassy) Avenida da Liberdade 198–200, 3rd floor; tel: 213 164 600; www.canadainternational.gc.ca/portugal.
UK (Embassy) Rua de São Bernardo 33; tel: 213-924 000; www.gov.uk/government/world/portugal.
US (Embassy) Avenida das Forças Armadas 16; tel: 217-273 300; https://pt.usembassy.gov.

Emergencies

Police, fire and ambulance tel: 112; tourist police tel: 213-400 090 and tel: 213-421 623.

Festivals and events

The following are just some of the main traditional festivals, but the Portuguese love an excuse for a party so expect myriad smaller events. Check out details with tourist information offices.
February or March Carnival – processions and fireworks.
March Moda Lisboa – Lisbon Fashion Week.
March–April Peixe em Lisboa – Fish Festival; Dias da Música em Belém – music festival at the Centro Cultural, Belém.

Easter parade

May IndieLisboa – Portugal's biggest independent film festival.
May–June Alkantara Art Festival; Rock in Rio (in even years) – five-day rock festival featuring international stars; Sintra Music Festival.
June Festas dos Santos Populares, including Festival of St Anthony, patron saint of Lisbon; Faz Música Lisboa – live music including blues, *fado*, jazz and rock in eight city venues.
July Nos Alive – an open-air rock, indie and pop festival (www.optimusalive.com); Superbock Superrock – mega rock festival; Sintra Music Festival.
August Jazz em Agosto – jazz concerts at the Gulbenkian open-air amphitheatre; Cascais Festas do Mar (Sea Festival) – ten days of music from pop and rock to *fado*; Estoril International Music Festival.
November Arte Lisboa – contemporary art fair; Lisbon and Sintra Film Festival.

Hours and holidays

Opening hours

Banks Mon–Fri 8.30am–3pm.
Museums and galleries the main closing day in Lisbon is Monday, otherwise most museums open all day.
Restaurants lunch noon–3pm, dinner 7–10pm or later. Many close for one day a week, often Sunday or Monday. Some close for part or the whole of August.
Shops Mon–Sat 9.30/10am–7pm, though some shut at 1pm on Saturday and a few of the smaller shops close for lunch. Shopping centres have very long hours, typically daily 10am to midnight, including Sunday.

Public holidays

Banks, offices and many shops and museums close on public holidays.
1 January Ano Novo (New Year's Day)
25 April Dia da Liberdade (1974 Revolution Day)
1 May Dia do Trabalhador (Labour Day)
10 June Dia de Camões (Camões's Day), also known as Portugal Day
15 August Assunção (Assumption)
5 October Implantação da República (Republic Day)
1 November Todos-os-Santos (All Saints' Day)
8 December Imaculada Conceição (Immaculate Conception)
25 December Natal (Christmas Day)
Moveable dates: Carnaval (Carnival/Shrove Tuesday), Sexta-feira Santa (Good Friday) and Corpo de Deus (Corpus Christi), ninth Thursday after Easter.

Lisbon, Estoril and Cascais have a local holiday on 13 June in honour of St Anthony (Santo António).

LGBTQ+ travellers

Lisbon is the most important city in Portugal's LGBTQ+ scene, offering plenty of bars and clubs

Flowers for sale on Rua Augusta

catering for a LGBTQ+ crowd. The scene centres around late-night gay bars in the Praça do Príncipe Real quarter, and also in nearby Bairro Alto. Out of Lisbon, at the south end of the Costa da Caparica, beach No 19 on the narrow-gauge railway is a very popular hangout.

A good queer travel website is www.patroc.com/lisbon, with information on hotels, bars, clubs, parties and events.

Other useful sites are www.lisbongaycircuit.com for bars, clubs, saunas and more, and www.portugalgay.pt for general information on gay life throughout Portugal. The Centro LGBTI (Rua dos Fanqueiros 40, Baixa; tel: 218-873 918) provides information and advice.

Media

Print media

British newspapers usually turn up on the same day as publication. The weekly *Portugal News*, (www.theportugalnews.com), published in the Algarve, is the country's main English-language paper and covers news and stories from around the country. Useful free Portuguese/English booklets include the monthly *Follow Me Lisboa*, packed with listings and other information, and *Lisboa Convida* in print and online (www.lisboa.convida.pt), a six-monthly shopping and leisure guide. They are available from tourist offices and some hotels.

TV and radio

Four television channels are widely available in Portugal, two of them state-run – RTP1 and RTP2 – and two privately owned, SIC and TVI. Foreign films are usually shown in the original language with subtitles. Most hotels have English-language channels such as BBC News and CNN.

Money

Currency

The euro (€) is the official currency used in Portugal. Notes are denominated in 5, 10, 20, 50, 100, 200 and 500 euros; coins in 1 and 2 euros and 1, 2, 5, 10, 20 and 50 cents.

Credit cards

Mastercard and Visa are the most widely accepted credit cards. Many places don't accept American Express. Some small shops and restaurants take cash only.

Cash machines

ATMs are widespread. You can normally take out a maximum of €400 a day.

Tipping and taxes

Tipping in Portugal is appreciated but not necessarily expected. However, leaving five to ten percent for good restaurant service is becoming more

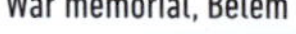

War memorial, Belém

common; in less formal establishments, locals often leave a euro or two. For taxis or in cafés, rounding up is plenty.

Religion

The Portuguese are predominantly Roman Catholic, a fact reflected in surviving religious rituals and saints' days that are public holidays. A service is held in English at 11.30am on Sunday at St George's (Anglican) Church in Estrela, at Rua São Jorge (www.lisbonanglicans.org).

Smoking

Smoking is still quite common in Portugal and a few restaurants and bars have dedicated smoking sections. Otherwise, smokers sit outside on the terrace. Smoking is banned on public transport and museums.

Telephones

Portugal's country code is 351. The local area code – 21 in the case of Lisbon and the Estoril Coast, including Sintra – must be dialled before all phone numbers, including local calls. To make an international call, dial 00 followed by the country code (UK 44, US 1, Australia 61, Canada and the US 1) plus the phone number including the area code, but without the initial 'O' where there is one. Following Brexit, some UK phone companies have withdrawn free mobile-phone roaming. To save on extortionate charges, buy an affordable local SIM card from one of the mobile network operators; Vodafone has an airport store.

Time zones

Mainland Portugal maintains Greenwich Mean Time (GMT), along with the UK, and is therefore one hour behind Spain. From the last Sunday in March until the last Sunday in October, the clocks are moved one hour ahead for summertime, GMT + 1. If it is noon in Lisbon, it will be 7am in New York, 1pm in Paris and 9pm in Sydney.

Toilets

Public toilets are limited but you can always stop for a *bica* in a bar or café. Normally, toilets are marked H for *homens* (men) or S for *senhoras* (women)

Tourist information

Lisbon has seventeen Ask Me Lisboa information points where you can buy the Lisboa Card (see Budgeting), book accommodation and pick up tourist information. The following are the main information points: Arrivals Hall, Lisbon Airport; tel: 218-450 660; daily 7am–midnight. Jardim Vasco da Gama, near the monastery in Belém; tel: 910-517 981; daily 9am–noon and 2–6pm; and another at Belém Tower; tel: 910-517 886; daily 9am–noon and 2–6pm. Praça do Comércio 78–81; tel: 914-081 366; daily 10am–8pm; and across

Fishing boats, Costa da Caparica

the square a second Ask Me Lisboa office; tel: 210-312 810; 9am–8pm.

Outside Lisbon

Sintra Ask Me Sintra, Praça da República 23 (in the town centre); tel: 219-231 157; daily 9.30am–6pm. There is also an office at the station; tel: 211-932 545; daily 9am–5pm.
Cascais Largo Cidade Vitória; tel: 912-034 214; daily 9am–6pm, summer until 8pm.

Tours and cruises

Some of the finest views of Lisbon are seen from the River Tagus. Lisboat (www.lisboat.com) has hop-on, hop-off boats and special cruises, including sunset *fado* trips. A single 48hr ticket enables you to jump from river to land and boat to bus, at your own pace.

More expensive but very special are the two-hour, all-year sailing cruises, organised by Tagus Cruises (www.taguscruises.com; tel: 925 610 034; minimum two people). Yachts set sail from Doca do Bom Sucesso close to Belém tower and floa past riverside landmarks, affording fine views of Cristo Rei, Ponte 25 de Abril, the Torre de Belém and other monuments as far as Alfama. Best of all are the sunset tours, where you sit back with a glass of wine as you watch the sun sink below the suspension bridge. For a more budget-friendly Tagus sailing experience, utilise the five public ferry routes.

Transport

Getting to Lisbon

Arrival by air
Lisbon's two-terminal airport is linked by scheduled daily non-stop flights to multiple European cities; the east and west coasts of the United States; and Canada. Flights from Australia and New Zealand route via London or another European capital. TAP/Air Portugal (www.flytap.com) is Portugal's national airline and has wide international links, including the US. Regular TAP flights connect Lisbon with London Gatwick and Heathrow. British Airways (www.ba.com) operates scheduled services from London Heathrow. Budget airlines offering direct services between the UK and Lisbon include easyJet (www.easyjet.com), with flights to/from Gatwick, Luton, Manchester, Bristol and Edinburgh, and Ryanair (ryanair.com), from London Stansted and Manchester. From Ireland, direct flights operate from Dublin with Aer Lingus and Ryanair.
Lisbon Airport (www.aeroportolisboa.pt) is just five miles (8km) northeast of the city and is well served by metro, bus and taxi. Terminal One is the terminus of the metro's red line. Trains operate from 6.30am–1am, but you will have to change at Alameda for Baixa. Alternatively, Carris public buses serve the airport and can provide more direct, if slower, connections.

Beach hut at Praia da Saúde

Both terminals have dedicated zones for rideshares, including Uber and Bolt. A free shuttle runs regularly between the two terminals.

Arrival by sea and rail

Lisbon is a major port, and several cruise ships include a call in the capital. Portugal's rail links with Spain and Europe beyond are slow and involve multiple changes – buses, including overnight services, are often preferable to reach Lisbon. It's hoped the night train connection between Madrid and Lisbon will be reinstated in late 2025.

Buses and trams

The bus and tram network, operated by Carris (www.carris.pt), covers virtually the whole city. Rush hour is notoriously busy so expect long waits. The website has detailed information on routes, schedules and maps. Buses are yellow and usually operate between 6.30am and midnight. A *paragem* is a bus stop. For tickets see Budgeting. Note that tickets must be validated in the machine on the bus or tram.

There are two types of tram: the charming vintage models and the new longer ones with sleek interiors. Trams operate in a limited area of the city. The most popular (and crowded) tourist tram is the No 28 (see Tour 9), which runs via Estrela, Bairro Alto/ Chiado, Baixa and the castle. Most trams are entered at the front, where you can buy a ticket from the driver or validate your pre-paid ticket.

Funiculars and lifts

Funiculars and lifts can save legwork on the city's hills. They are included in a one-day transport pass or Viva Viagem card; otherwise, they are expensive for what is a very short ride.

Metro

Lisbon's underground Metropolitano (www.metrolisboa.pt) has four colour-coded lines (red, green, yellow and blue) and is easy to use. The service operates from 6.30am until 1am. The red line links the city to the airport. Certain stations connect with the railway stations and ferry termini. The cheapest way to travel is to buy an electronic Viva Viagem card, available at metro vending machines and ticket offices, which you then charge up as you go (see Budgeting), though contactless payments are easier and only marginally more expensive.

Trains (comboios)

Lisbon has four railway stations. The main ones for national travel are Santa Apolónia and Estação do Oriente. Commuter trains for the western suburbs, Estoril and Cascais depart from Cais do Sodré about every twenty minutes, and take thirty minutes, while trains for Sintra depart from Rossio station, also every twenty minutes (journey time forty minutes). The national rail company is CP (Comboios de Portugal), which connects the capital to the major cities of the country.

Time Out Mercado da Ribeira

Taxis

Taxis are cheap by European standards. Most are black and green. Taxi ranks can be found at main squares and stations but can also be hailed in the street. The fare is shown on the meter – check that it's running before you set off. There are extra charges from 9pm until 6am and at weekends, and for luggage placed in the boot. To order a taxi: Teletáxis: 218-111 100; Autocoope: 217-932 756.

Ferries

The two main ferry stations for the River Tagus's southern shore are Estação Fluvial Terreiro do Paço for Barreiro and Cais do Sodré for Cacilhas, Montijo and Seixal.

By bike and scooter

Given Lisbon's hilly terrain, uneven streets and traffic-filled lanes, few tourists choose to hire a bike, or if they do, it's an electric one. The areas you might consider cycling include the riverside track from Cais do Sodré to Belém (and Belém itself, which is very flat), and Parque das Naçôes, where bikes can be hired. Lisbon Cycle Tours (lisboncycletours.com) offers an excellent three-hour seven-hills tour on e-bikes showing you parts of the city most tourists don't explore.

Since 2018, electric scooters are found everywhere. Lime is the biggest rental company. To hire one, download the company app and register, find a scooter on the street (or via the card in the app) and unlock it by scanning the QR code. You can leave the scooter anywhere (except the red zones of Alfama and Bairro Alto) but be sure to click 'end ride' and take a picture to give more information to the next renter. Scooters are easy to ride, fun and fast (up to 27km/h on the flat) but quite pricey if you compare them with Uber or public transport. They are best on flat, paved surfaces, and not ideal for steep, cobbled streets.

Car hire

Major international firms such as Avis, Hertz, Europcar and Budget have desks at the airport and locations in Lisbon, but for the best deals, book online in advance. EV (electric vehicle) rentals are growing in popularity, though most companies offer hybrid, rather than exclusively electric, cars. The minimum age for hiring a car is 21 to 25 (depending on the company), and the driver must have held a valid licence for at least a year – the exception being OK Mobility, which rents to new drivers. Hire companies will accept your home country's national driving license, but you must show your passport. Third-party insurance should be included in the basic charge. All rental contracts in Portugal have excess amounts of around €1000. The cost to waive the excess can be upwards of €20 a day; it is far cheaper to take out an excess insurance policy in advance.

In the arcades flanking Praça do Comércio

Driving

Try to avoid driving in Lisbon. Roads are narrow and frequently congested, signage is almost non-existent, and parking is near-impossible in the historic centre. For most visitors, public transport and inexpensive private taxis are vastly superior ways to navigate the city. There is also an excellent train service to Cascais and Sintra, and buses to Óbidos, Mafra and Sesimbra. However, a car is very useful for exploring the Alentejo region or the Serra da Arrábida. EV-charging points are becoming more common in Lisbon, Sintra, Setúbal and Mafra; some hotels have dedicated chargers – www.electromaps.com is a good resource for locating stations.

To bring your own car into Portugal you will need your national driving licence, registration papers and insurance. The main roads of Portugal are generally in good repair.

Rules and regulations

The rules of the road are the same as in most Western European countries. Drive on the right. At roundabouts, the vehicle already on the roundabout has priority unless road markings or lights indicate otherwise. Seat belts are compulsory, and a heavy fine can be imposed if you are not wearing one.

Speed limits are 120km/h (75mph) on motorways, 100km/h (62.5mph) on roads restricted to motor vehicles, 90km/h (56mph) on other roads, 50km/h (37mph) in urban areas and 50km/h (31mph) in special zones. Most motorways and the Ponte 25 de Abril have tolls.

Visas and passports

The long-delayed ETIAS (European Travel Information and Authorisation System) visa waiver for non-EU passport holders is set to finally be introduced in 2025. Costing €7, it will be valid for several years and will allow holders to travel to the EU without a visa for up to ninety days in any 180-day period. All travellers will require a passport that has at least six months of validity remaining at the date of entry to the EU (see www.gov.uk/renew-adult-passport/renew). EU citizens only require a valid passport or identity card to enter Portugal for trips of up to ninety days. For longer stays, a visa or residence permit is required.

Websites

www.visitlisboa.com – official tourist office site for Lisbon.
www.visitportugal.com – official tourism site for Portugal.
www.carris.pt – public transport website.
www.cp.pt – Caminhos de Portugal, the railway network.
www.theportugalnews.com – national newspaper in English.

A tourist sightseeing bus

Language

Portuguese is the sixth most spoken language in the world with around 220 million native speakers and 260 million total speakers. Any school Spanish may help with signs and menus, but will not unlock the mysteries of spoken Portuguese, with its many nasal sounds. Almost all hotels have staff who speak English and unless you go off the beaten track you should have little problem communicating in most shops or restaurants. Almost everyone understands Spanish and many speak French, but just learning a few simple words and phrases in Portuguese will certainly enhance your visit and help if you are off the tourist circuit. Here are a few basics to help you get started.

General

hello (good morning) *bom dia*
good afternoon/evening *boa tarde*
good night *boa noite*
goodbye *adeus*
yes *sim*
no *não*
thank you *obrigado (masc) obrigada (fem)*
many thanks *muito obrigado*
you're welcome *de nada*
please *faz favor, por favor*
I need... *preciso...*
I'm sorry *desculpe-me*
excuse me *com licença*
I don't know *não sei*
I don't understand *não comprendo*
do you speak English? French *fala inglês? francês?*
please speak slowly *faz favor de falar devagar*
please say that again *diga outra vez, se faz favor*
how much does it cost? *quanto custa?*

At a bar/restaurant

have you got a table for....... *tem uma mesa para?*
may we have the menu? *a ementa se faz favor*
what do you recommend? *que recomenda?*
fixed-price menu *a ementa turística*
what wine do you recommend? *qual é o vinho que recomenda?*
mineral water (still) *agua sem gás; (fizzy) agua com gás*
red (mature)/white wine ("green") *vinho tinto (maduro)/branco (verde)*
bottle/half bottle *garrafa/ meia garrafa*
beer *cerveja*
cheers! *saúde!*
do you take credit cards? *aceitam cartões de credito?*
the bill please *a conta se faz favor*
toilets (ladies/gents, men/ women) *casa de banho (senhoras/ senhores, homens/mulheres)*

Azulejo signage

Numbers

1 *um/uma*
2 *dois/duas*
3 *três*
4 *quatro*
5 *cinco*
6 *seis*
7 *sete*
8 *oito*
9 *nove*
10 *dez*
20 *vinte*
30 *trinta*
40 *quarenta*
50 *cinquenta*
100 *cem*
1,000 *mil*

Getting around

how do I get to…? *como se vai para…?*
where is…? *onde é…?*
left/right *esquerda/direita*
straight on *sempre em frente*
what time do you open/ close? *a que hora abre/fecha?*
can you help me? *pode ajudar-me?*
can you show me? *pode mostrar me?*
I'm lost *estou perdido/a*
can we walk there? *podemos ir a pé?*
railway station *estação de comboio*
bus station *estação de autocarros*
train *comboio*
return ticket *bilhete de ida e volta*
single ticket *bilhete de ida*
ticket office *bilheteria*

Days of the week

Sunday *domingo*
Monday *segunda-feira*
Tuesday *terça-feira*
Wednesday *quarta-feira*
Thursday *quinta-feira*
Friday *sexta-feira*
Saturday *sábado*
Today *hoje*
Yesterday *ontem*
Tomorrow *amanhã*

Online

Where is an internet café?
Onde fica um Internet café?
Can I access the internet here?
Tenho acesso à internet aqui?
What is the WiFi password?
Qual é a senha do WiFi?
Is the WiFi free? *O WiFi é grátis?*
How do I log on/log off?
Como faço o logon/logoff?
Can I..? *Posso..?*
What's your email? *Qual é o seu e-mail?*
My email is.... *O meu e-mail é.....*
To print *imprimir*

Social media

Are you on Facebook/Twitter?
Esta no Facebook/Twitter?
What's your user name? *Qual é o seu nome de utilizador?*
I'll add you as a friend *Vou adicioná-lo como amigo*
I'll follow you on Twitter
Vou segui-lo no Twitter
I'll put the pictures on Facebook/Twitter *Vou colocar as fotos no Facebook/Twitter*

Newspapers for sale

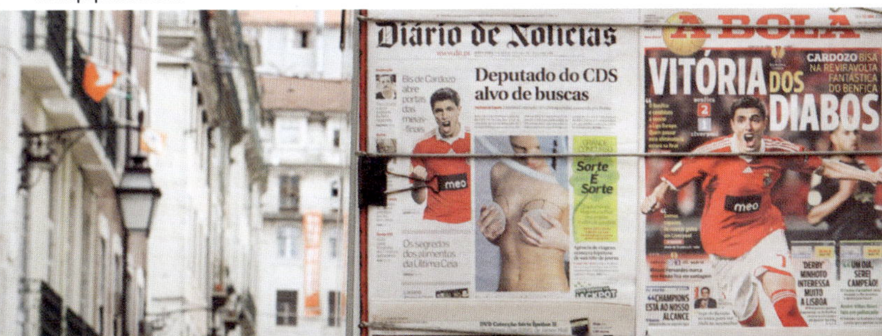

Books and film

Lisbon has attracted foreign writers for several centuries. In 1754 Henry Fielding, author of *Tom Jones*, came here for his health but died two months' later (he is buried in the city's English cemetery). By the end of the eighteenth century, grand tours were beginning to attract romantic imaginations. The most famous visitors included William Beckford, who lived near Sintra, and Byron, Southey and Keats, who were all also inspired by Sintra. Byron was not always complimentary about Portugal. In his epic poem, *Childe Harold*, the Portuguese – described as 'Lusian brute' – are picked out for special attack. George Borrow, the intrepid nineteenth-century author and Bible salesman who travelled to Portugal in 1835, has left to posterity some wonderfully descriptive accounts of his journeys.

A good number of books on Portugal are available in English, and the list below is just a tiny selection.

Portuguese writers

Luís de Camões Portugal's great national poet, author of the great epic poem, *The Lusiads*, written in 1572 and describing Vasco da Gama's discovery of the sea route to India.
Eça de Queirós (1845–1900) is Portugal's leading realist writer of the nineteenth century, often ranked alongside Balzac and Dickens. His most popular work is *The Maias*.
Eugénio Lisboa has edited a number of books of poetry and short stories, including *The Anarchist Banker and Other Portuguese Stories*, and *Professor Pfiglzz and His Strange Companion*.
Fernando Pessoa (1888–1935) is second only to Camões in the list of illustrious Portuguese poets. He wrote under other names: Alberto Caeiro, Ricardo Reis and Álvaro de Campos, transforming his style with each. His *Book of Disquiet* contains his disturbing meditations around Chiado.
José Saramago (1922–2010) received the Nobel Prize for Literature in 1998. *Journey to Portugal: In Pursuit of Portugal's History and Culture* is a wonderful travelogue.
Miguel Torga's autobiography, *The Creation of the World* recalls his Trás-os-Montes childhood in northern Portugal, his boyhood in Brazil and the return to his native village to work as a doctor.

Books about Portugal

Non-fiction

A Concise History of Portugal by David Birmingham. A standard history book regaling the heritage of Portugal, with many illustrations.

Nobel Prize award winner José Saramago

Backwards Out of the Big World: A Voyage into Portugal by Paul Hyland. Following in the steps of Henry Fielding from Lisbon to the Spanish border.

The First Global Village: How Portugal Changed the World by Martin Page. A comprehensive and very readable history by a journalist with a deep knowledge of the city and its people.

The Last Day: Wrath, Ruin and Reason in the Great Lisbon Earthquake of 1755 by Nicholas Shrady. Riveting history of the earthquake and the shock waves it sent throughout western civilisation.

Portuguese Voyages 1498–1663 edited by Charles David Ley. Tales from the Great Age of Discovery, drawn from contemporary accounts.

Republican Portugal, a Political History 1910–1926 by Douglas L. Wheeler. A fascinating account of the period between monarchy and dictatorship when Portugal endured 45 successive governments.

They Went to Portugal by Rose Macaulay. A lively account of Lisbon's visitors, mainly British, from the Crusaders to the romantic writers of the nineteenth century.

Fiction

The Last Kabbalist of Lisbon by Richard Zimler. Historical thriller set in Lisbon in 1506, when 'New Christian' Jewish converts were being murdered.

The Migrant Painter of Birds by Lidia Jorge. A beautifully crafted poetic novel about a girl from a Portuguese farming family and her absent father.

A Small Death in Lisbon by Robert Wilson. Compelling award-winning thriller with plots intertwining between Portugal in World War II and the 1990s.

Films

The Lovers of Lisbon (1955). French film based on the novel *Les Amants du Tage*. Two French exiles in Lisbon who have both murdered their spouses fall in love.

Lisbon (1956). A US adventure romance, where an American smuggler is hired to rescue a wealthy industrialist who is a prisoner behind the Iron Curtain.

Pereira Declares (1996). The political awakening of a cautious journalist, Dr Pereira (played by Marcello Mastroianni) during the Salazar dictatorship. Based on the eponymous book by Antonio Tabucchi.

Night Train to Lisbon (2013). Directed by Bille August and starring Jeremy Irons, the film is based on the European bestselling novel, *Night Train to Lisbon*, by Pascar Mercier.

Haircut (2014). Independent postmodern Portuguese filmdirected by Joaquim Sapinho, examining crisis and compromise in the relationship of a young couple in the 1990s.

For cinematic tours of Lisbon visit www.lisbonmovietour.com.

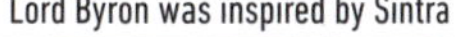

Lord Byron was inspired by Sintra

About this book

The Rough Guides Walks & Tours series helps you discover the world's most exciting destinations through our expert-curated trip plans: a range of walks and tours designed to suit all budgets, interests and trip lengths. These walks, driving tours and site excursions cover the destination's most quintessential attractions as well as a range of lesser-known sights, while food and drink stops for refreshments en route are highlighted in boxes. If you're not sure which walk to pick, our Best walks & tours for... feature suggests which ones work best for particular interests. The introduction provides a destination overview, while the directory supports the walks and tours with all the essential information you need, as well as our pick of where to stay while you are there and select restaurant listings, to complement the more low-key options given in the trip plans.

About the authors

Susie Boulton fell in love with Portugal as a child, assisting her grandmother on a water divining mission in the Algarve before the tidal wave of tourism. She wrote her first guidebook to Lisbon in 1992 and has seen the city change from what felt like a relatively remote outpost to one of the most exciting capitals in Europe. As a freelance travel writer, Susie has written around thirty guidebooks to European destinations. **Daniel Stables** is a travel writer based in Manchester, UK. He writes travel articles for National Geographic and the BBC, and his debut narrative travel book, Fiesta: A Journey Through Festivity is coming out in early 2026. He also hosts a podcast, Hungry Ghosts, about food and travel. You can find his work on X @ DanStables, Instagram @DanStabs, or via his website, danielstables.co.uk.

Help us update

We've gone to a lot of effort to ensure that this edition of the **Rough Guides Walks & Tours Lisbon** is accurate and up-to-date. However, things change – places get "discovered", new gems open up, restaurants and rooms raise prices or lower standards. If you feel we've got it wrong or left something out, we'd like to know, and if you can remember the address, the website, whether or not it was free to enter – so much the better.

Please send your comments with the subject line "**Rough Guides Walks & Tours Lisbon Update**" to mail@roughguides.com. We'll acknowledge all contributions and send a copy of the next edition (or any other Rough Guide if you prefer) for the very best emails.

Credits

Rough Guides Walks & Tours Lisbon
Editor: Joanna Reeves
Original author: Susie Boulton
Updater: Daniel Stables
Picture Editor: Piotr Kala
Picture Manager: Tom Smyth
Cartography: Katie Bennett
Layout: Grzegorz Madejak
Production Operations Manager: Katie Bennett
Publishing Technology Manager: Rebeka Davies
Head of Publishing: Sarah Clark
Photo credits: All images Shutterstock except: Bigstock 67; Design Hotels 108; Four Seasons Hotels 110, 111; Heritage Lisbon Hotels/Telmo Miller 114; iStock 7M, 38, 40, 41R, 51R, 59, 61, 70, 71T, 81R, 83B, 84, 91, 101T, 120, 134; Leonardo 107, 109, 112, 115; Lydia Evans/Apa Publications 6ML, 6BC, 7T, 7MR, 7MR, 11R, 13, 16/17, 17R, 18, 19, 20, 20/21, 21R, 30, 30/31, 31R, 32, 33, 34, 40/41, 42, 44, 45, 46, 46/47, 47R, 48, 49, 52, 65R, 64/65, 77, 80B, 80T, 83T, 85, 86, 87, 88B, 88T, 88/89, 89R, 90, 94, 97, 105T, 118, 121, 124, 125, 126, 127, 128, 129, 130, 131, 132, 133, 135; PortoBay Hotels & Resorts 113; Public domain 24, 25, 52/53; Turismo de Lisboa 4BL, 4MR, 4BR
Cover credits: Tram **iStock**

Printed by Finidr in Czech Republic

This book was produced using **Typefi** automated publishing software.

A catalogue record for this book is available from the British Library.

First Edition 2025

ISBN: 9781835292594

Distribution

UK, Ireland and Europe
Apa Publications (UK) Ltd; mail@roughguides.com
United States and Canada
Two Rivers; ips@ingramcontent.com
Australia and New Zealand
Woodslane; info@woodslane.com.au
Worldwide
Apa Publications (UK) Ltd; mail@roughguides.com

Special Sales, Content Licensing and CoPublishing

Rough Guides can be purchased in bulk quantities at discounted prices. We can create special editions, personalized jackets and corporate imprints tailored to your needs.
mail@roughguides.com
http://roughguides.com

EU Representative

LOGOS EUROPE, 9 rue Nicolas Poussin, 17000, LA ROCHELLE, France
Contact@logoseurope.eu
+33 (0) 667937378

Index

MAP LEGEND

Start of tour
Tour & route direction
Recommended sight
Recommended restaurant/café
Place of interest
Tourist information
Railway
Motorway
Ferry route
Main bus station
Metro station
Main post office
Statue/monument
Museum/gallery
Theatre
Airport
Lighthouse
Beach
Cave
Viewpoint
Castle / ruin
Church
Monastery
Palace
Important building
Park
Pedestrian area
Urban area
Non-urban area
Transport hub